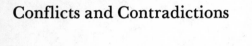

Conflicts and Contradictions

ORGANIZATIONAL AND OCCUPATIONAL PSYCHOLOGY

Series Editor: PETER WARR
MRC/SSRC Social and Applied Psychology Unit, Department of Psychology, The University, Sheffield, England

Theodore D. Weinshall
Managerial Communication: Concepts, Approaches and Techniques, 1979

Chris Argyris
Inner Contradictions of Rigorous Research, 1980

Charles J. de Wolff, Sylvia Shimmin, and Maurice de Montmollin
Conflicts and Contradictions: Work Psychology in Europe, 1981

In preparation
J. D. Cook, S. J. Hepworth, T. D. Wall and P. B. Warr
The Experience of Work: A Compendium and
Review of 249 Measures and Their Use

Nigel Nicholson, Gill Ursell and Paul Blyton
The Dynamics of White Collar Unionism

Conflicts and Contradictions

Work Psychologists in Europe

CHARLES J. DE WOLFF
University of Nijmegen
SYLVIA SHIMMIN
University of Lancaster
and
MAURICE DE MONTMOLLIN
University of Paris-Nord

with contributions from
Marian Dobrzyński, Göran Ekvall, Milton D. Hakel, Frank A. Heller,
Heinz-Ludwig Horney, Michèle Lacoste, Jacques Naymark,
Enzo Spaltro, Jean-Claude Sperandio

1981

ACADEMIC PRESS
A Subsidiary of Harcourt Brace Jovanovich, Publishers
LONDON   NEW YORK   TORONTO   SYDNEY   SAN FRANCISCO

Academic Press Inc. (London) Ltd
24–28 Oval Road
London NW1

US edition published by
Academic Press Inc.
111 Fifth Avenue,
New York, New York 10003

British Library Cataloguing in Publication Data

Conflicts and contradictions. — (Organizational
and occupational psychology).
1. Psychology, Industrial
I. De Wolff, C J   II. Shimmin, S
III. De Montmollin, M   IV. Series
158.7   HF5548.8   80-41633

ISBN 0-12-214650-6

Typeset by Dobbie Typesetting Service, Plymouth, Devon
Printed by T. J. Press (Padstow) Ltd., Padstow, Cornwall

Contributors

The various contributors to this volume are introduced at appropriate places in the text. Their normal addresses for correspondence are listed below.

MAURICE DE MONTMOLLIN
3 Avenue de Stalingrad, 91120 Palaiseau, France

CHARLES J. DE WOLFF
Katholieke Universiteit, Montessorilaan 3, Box 9104, 6500 HE Nijmegen, The Netherlands

MARIAN DOBRZYŃSKI
Dunikowskiego 4m7, 02 784 Warsaw, Poland

GÖRAN EKVALL
PA rådet, Sturegatan 58, Box 5157, 102 44 Stockholm, Sweden

MILTON D. HAKEL
Department of Psychology, The Ohio State University, 404C West 17th Avenue, Columbus, Ohio 43210, USA

FRANK A. HELLER
The Tavistock Institute of Human Relations, The Tavistock Centre, Belsize Lane, London NW3 5BA, England

HEINZ-LUDWIG HORNEY
Am alten Stadtpark 55, 4630 Bochum 1, West Germany

MICHÈLE LACOSTE
Laboratoire Communication et Travail, Université Paris-Nord, Avenue J.B. Clément, 93430 Villetaneuse, France

JACQUES NAYMARK
13 Rue des Cinq Diamants, 75013 Paris, France

SYLVIA SHIMMIN
Department of Behaviour in Organisations, The University of Lancaster, Gillow House, Bailrigg, Lancaster LA1 4YX, England

ENZO SPALTRO
Instituto Politico-Amministrativo, Via Giuseppe Petroni 33, Bologna 40126, Italy

JEAN-CLAUDE SPERANDIO
27ter Avenue Albert 1, 94210 La Varenne, France

Preface

Every book has its own story and this book is no exception. Usually the story is not told in the book because the author thinks it is of no interest to readers or that it is none of their business. When the story is told, it is narrated to relatives and close friends and then only part of it. A psychology book normally presents theories, research findings and scientific discussions and states in the preface that it is written because it might be of interest to other psychologists, other professionals, laypeople or to meet particular teaching needs.

Amongst psychologists (and they are not the only ones) there is a distinct difference between written and oral communication. In our books and journals we present the results of our studies and our theories and we review and appraise the publications of others. This is done in carefully phrased language and it usually takes a lot of time to prepare the contributions. In oral communication, however, we exchange gossip, tell what happened in our work, express our concerns, criticize, lobby and try to influence. Both in content and expression there is little resemblance to what we write for publication.

This oral communication is very important. As any professional with experience knows, one cannot do a job without being a member of appropriate networks through which one learns much which never appears in writing and certainly not in scientific journals. Occasionally a president refers to this type of material in a presidential address and some letters appear in the journals of professional associations about issues arising from oral communication. Otherwise, little of what is transmitted orally is available to those who were not involved in the particular group or network.

This book is the product of a group activity. In 1973 one of the authors was invited by the late Rains Wallace, editor of the American journal *Personnel Psychology*, to write a review about industrial psychology in Europe. After giving it some thought he decided that this would be an impossible thing to do. Industrial psychology in Europe is not a unity and can in no way be compared to industrial psychology in the United States. There are about twenty different countries, and more than twenty languages. Most countries have their own professional association and the exchange of information is rather limited. Some European psychologists have the feeling that they know more about what is going on in the United States than about what happens in a neighbouring country.

After some discussions it was decided that he should try to set up a group of industrial psychologists to prepare the review. It was thought that a group would give a better idea of developments in Europe than an individual author. As a result of a chance meeting with Dr. Lynn Baker in London, who expressed interest in the project, a travel grant was provided to enable members of the group to get together. The establishment of this group is a story in itself, but we will be brief about it here. Charles de Wolff, who knew a number of people abroad, initiated the process. Through consultation, and also with a lot of good luck, he managed to establish a group of seven psychologists, all from different countries, covering the main areas of Europe. Since 1974 this group, Marian Dobrzyński, Göran Ekvall, Heinz-Ludwig Horney, Maurice de Montmollin, Sylvia Shimmin, Enzo Spaltro and Charles de Wolff, has met once or twice a year, usually in Europe but on two occasions in the United States. All members of the group participated in a symposium at the 1976 APA convention in Washington, following the publication that year of the original review in *Personnel Psychology*.

Through many discussions we became aware of our own professional positions and of the value of continuing our meetings. We also wanted to share our ideas with a wider audience and conceived the idea of this book. Many of the issues we write about are problematic, but we have found that they can be explored by comparing and contrasting the situations and activities in different countries. Having said this, we recognize that the informal exchange and dialogue referred to above cannot be reproduced in written form, so what is presented here is only a distillation of some of the discussions. Furthermore, as both authors and readers are conditioned by traditions and conventions of presentation and format, the content of this book is inevitably more like conventional written communication. But its origins lie in oral communication, which is reflected in some of the contributions. Consequently some people will undoubtedly point out that the views expressed ought to be better documented and supported by research. However, as with much oral communication, there is a lack of empirical evidence or, if it exists, we are not aware of it.

To some extent our group represents the psychological establishment in our respective countries. We are all university professors, with wide experience of teaching, research and consultancy, have written books and articles in the field, are members of the editorial boards of a number of journals, hold or have held important positions in national and international professional organizations, have served on all kinds of advisory bodies, i.e. we belong to the "dominant faction", as we will argue later, and thus contribute to the shaping of the profession. All of us identify clearly with the professional side of our activities, and share a concern about the standards of quality and the further development of the profession. This is reflected in the conscious choice to occupy academic positions, rather than to enter, say, personnel management, commercial consultancy or university administration. Possibly we exert more influence than we realize on the perception, values and development of the profession in our respective countries. But this should not be taken as indicating that our ideas necessarily represent those of our colleagues in the psychological establishment. While we value the importance of scientific work, and try to contribute to it and stimulate others to do so, our experience of application leads us to question some of the underlying assumptions of traditional psychological education and training and the activities of the professional associations in this respect. We do not even share a unitary view amongst ourselves. Some of us are probably more at the rebel end of the continuum of opinions in our country, while others are closer to the conformist position, e.g. one of us has gone on record as saying that, in his opinion, the future of industrial psychology lies outside the field of academic psychology and he now teaches in an engineering department. It will be apparent that we cannot claim to speak for the profession as a whole, either in national or international terms. However, we feel confident that our ideas will be of interest, both to those who agree and those who disagree with us, and we hope it will stimulate discussions of the type we have found so useful.

In preparing this book, three members of the group have undertaken the major responsibility of writing and editing. This is partly due to the differing facility with which members write in English, our common working language, and also to geographical factors which make it easier for some to meet together. Nevertheless everyone has contributed in one way or another. Charles de Wolff and Sylvia Shimmin are joint authors of Section 1, in which they describe the development of the domain and the emergence of the profession of work psychology. This section ends by raising some of the problems of professional practice in the field. They have also edited Section 2, which is contributed by a number of authors who do not usually publish in English and who illustrate the themes described in Section 1 in the setting of six different countries. The task of putting these papers into colloquial English has been undertaken largely by Sylvia Shimmin. Section 3 is edited by Maurice de Montmollin; he also contributes to it as an author. In particular, he has included a number of papers by French authors which show the somewhat differing climate in which work psychologists operate in France. Section 4 is the product of the three authors, in which an attempt has been made to look into the future, not in the sense of predicting what will happen, but in suggesting a number of possibilities open to the profession as a whole.

November 1980

CHARLES DE WOLFF
SYLVIA SHIMMIN
MAURICE DE MONTMOLLIN

Contents

Section 3   Conflicts and Contradictions: Some Typical Positions
             edited by Maurice de Montmollin

Section 4   Future Trends
             *Charles J. de Wolff, Sylvia Shimmin
             and Maurice de Montmollin*

Section 1
The Domain of Work Psychology

CHARLES J. DE WOLFF and SYLVIA SHIMMIN

1 Work Psychology in Europe: The Development of a Profession

A. Subject area

The branch of psychology with which we are concerned is one which we shall designate as "the psychology of work". This is a subject area with no fixed boundaries and, indeed, in Europe there is no one term used to describe it. For example, in Britain the preferred term is still "occupational psychology", although some feel this is now obsolescent, whereas, on the mainland of Europe, "Psychotechnics" was formerly accepted but is now hardly ever used. 'The psychology of work and organizations" has largely superseded the older designation of "industrial psychology" for what, in the United States, is embraced by the comprehensive label of "industrial and organizational psychology (I/O psychology)". Whenever possible, we shall refer to "the psychology of work" and to its practitioners as "work psychologists", but readers should note that other contributors may refer to the same area by other names, e.g. as "I/O psychology" or "occupational psychology".

One factor which has influenced recent developments is the awareness that psychology is not applied solely in industrial organizations and this, together with the growth of organizational theory, has led to a broad area of professional activities relating to work and organizations. As a result, traditional industrial psychology, associated with individual appraisal and vocational counselling, has become a subsection of an emergent professional field which includes

3

selection, organizational psychology, training, human factors and personnel research. Organizations of all kinds — employers, trade unions, government bodies — have come to recognize and express a need for contributions from this emerging field. This has required that "work psychologists" change their approach from one based on attaining the best fit between the individual and his job, in which the technology is taken for granted, to one which takes account of the organization as a whole and the social, political environment in which it operates.

B.   Historical background

The psychology of work is commonly thought to be of recent origin, but in many European countries there was pioneering work by a few individuals much earlier. To name but a few examples:

1889 L. O. Patrizi founded a Laboratory of Work Psychology in Modena, Italy

1908 Lahy studied work design and selection for railways engineers in France

1918 The Industrial Fatigue Research Board was established in England

1919 Selection testing programmes were started by Walter Moede, in Germany, and Franziska Baumgarten, in Switzerland

1920 The Institute for Psychotechnics was established at Krakow in Poland

Further details of developments in the twenties are given by Spaltro (1974), Leplat (1971) and Baumgarten-Tramer (1971). This was a fruitful period in Europe, with much cross-national collaboration. In contrast, the nineteen thirties was a decade of little growth. A contributory factor, particularly in Germany, was the clash between the German Psychological Association and the Nazi Government, as a result of which many psychologists left to work in other countries, particularly the USA. Similarly the period of the second world war saw few significant developments, except in Britain where the work of psychologists was highly related to manpower requirements in a period of emergency. The impact of this work was seen in developments in the immediate post-war period, during which the Tavistock Institute of

Human Relations was established, and the Civil Service Selection Board adopted assessment methods based on War Office Selection procedures. However, most of the activities before 1947, especially on the mainland of Europe, were on a relatively small scale and individualistic.

Since 1947 the growth of psychology throughout Europe has been extensive. Formal training programmes at universities and independent research groups were started, some of which continue to grow. Even in Britain, where there were some degree programmes prior to 1940, several new departments of psychology were created after the war. In addition, there has been a great increase in the number of polytechnics and schools of business or management in which psychology forms a component of training programmes. From the early nineteen sixties onwards the number of young people entering universities and other institutes of higher education expanded rapidly, of whom a significant proportion were attracted to the social sciences. Consequently the study of psychology has become very popular. Taking the discipline as a whole, the number of students graduating each year shows an exponential growth, with no sign of waning. Although the rate of growth varies between countries the number of psychologists has doubled every five to seven years.

The psychology of work has also expanded considerably over the same period, but its rate of growth has been linear rather than exponential. Figure 1., based on a Dutch study (Krijnen, 1976), illustrates this clearly. Although comparable statistics from other European countries are not readily available, we believe that the trends shown in Fig. 1 apply to them also. What it reflects, among other things, is the impact of the ideological debate about power, authority and the nature of society, which reached a climax at the end of the nineteen sixties, and which led psychology students to avoid work psychology, lest they were seen as aligned with the establishment. In the late nineteen seventies, the position is less clear-cut. Some of us have the impression that student attitudes may now be changing, but it is still too early to tell what effects these may have on the projected numbers of work psychologists.

C. Some illustrative data

In the absence of official statistics, the number of students and of

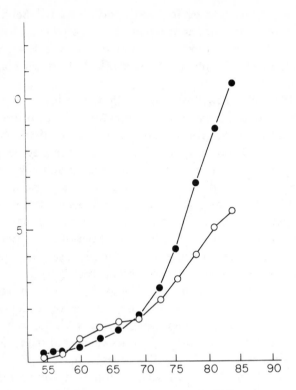

Until 1975 actual growth; after 1975 forecast

FIG. 1 Rate of growth of psychologists and work psychologists in the Netherlands. ●, Total × 1000; ○, work psychologists × 100.

practising psychologists in different countries is difficult to estimate. Furthermore, the figures which are available have to be seen in the light of the population as a whole. There are also differences between countries as to the definitions of qualified psychologists, e.g. some people are employed in work of an applied psychological nature who have not completed the full cycle of their studies. The following data have been mainly provided by members of our group, from sources in their own countries, but they are presented here solely to indicate the patterns of interest and employment in Europe, and should not be taken out of context.

Scandinavian countries: We have some data for Sweden (8 million inhabitants). There is a rapid growth in the number of psychology students, but almost ninety per cent of these are aiming to become psychotherapists. Courses in behavioural science have been developed for those intending to work in personnel administration. Sweden is commonly perceived as the country in Europe where work psychology is most developed and the projects on participation and work structuring are widely known.

We have no figures for Norway and Denmark but the situation is roughly comparable to Sweden.

United Kingdom: (population 56 million). Traditional industrial psychology was established relatively early and contributed to the development of the field through some well-known studies, e.g. those of the Industrial Health Research Board in the inter-war period. This type of work is now in decline and the extent to which industrial and organizational psychology is becoming established in its place is problematic. As elsewhere, there are now many practitioners in the organizational field with qualifications other than in psychology, e.g. industrial sociologists and graduates from business schools. Students in large numbers seek entrance to psychology undergraduate courses; but not all of them intend to practise as psychologists when they graduate. The psychology of work tends to be taught as an undergraduate option, rather than as a compulsory course, although in certain universities it is central to the programme. In contrast with clinical psychologists, for which there are clear career structures and an associated programme of professional training, work psychologists enter a diversity of jobs, some of which require no specialized training in the subject. At the end of 1979 the total membership of the British Psychological Society was 7130 (as compared to 811 in 1941) of whom approximately 600 were occupational psychologists. These figures are less than the actual numbers of university trained psychologists in the population because it is not mandatory for them to join the society.

The Netherlands (population 14 million). As indicated earlier, Krijnen undertook a systematic study of the developments in psychology which was published in 1975 and 1976. The position in this country is therefore better documented than that in the rest of Europe. Compared to most other countries, the proportion of work psychologists is higher and their employment position is more firmly established. In the early post-war period some large companies and organizations in the public sector started their own psychological departments, where work psychologists were engaged mainly in selection work. Thus, unlike their European counterparts, a considerate percentage of Dutch work psychologists have been employed by business and public organizations (e.g. in 1963 this was 28%). When, during the nineteen sixties, the Universities grew enormously in size, educational and research institutes became the most important employers (totalling 52% in 1972). Since the early nineteen seventies this section has begun to lose its prominence — and it will continue to do so in the years ahead. In the study by Krijnen, both psychologists and informed observers who were interviewed were rather optimistic about future employment opportunities. Although there is now some unemployment among psychologists (500 at the end of 1979), those who graduate as work psychologists do not experience particular problems in obtaining posts, e.g. only 8 were unemployed at the end of 1979. Student interest in the discipline of psychology as a whole continues to increase, although clinical and social psychology are the most popular subjects. The total number of students is now over 9000, with the universities admitting about 1800 students per year. Relatively speaking, the number of students selecting work psychology is small, but this can be misleading as it has been shown that psychologists who have chosen other specialities may move to work psychology at a later stage of the career, e.g. social psychologists.

Federal Republic of Germany: (population 61 million). In 1979 there were about 12 000 psychologists, of whom about 5000 were members of the German Association of Applied Psychology. In this association some 600 persons are members of the industrial and organizational division. As elsewhere, there is an enormous interest in psychology on the part of students, of whom there are about 17 000 pursuing the subject. This number would even be greater but for the *numerus fixus* of 2000 students per year which is enforced by the government. 80-90% of the students enter the field of clinical psychology. In recent years there has been a rise in the unemployment of professionally qualified psychologists, i.e. those holding the "diplom" degree. In 1977 there were some 600 unemployed psychologists, but this figure rose to 900 in 1978.

France: (population 53 million). At the beginning of 1978 there were about 29 000 students. Of this large number it is known that only a small proportion will complete the total programme — i.e. reach doctoral level — and become qualified as true practitioners. Many of these students are only studying on a part-time basis as they have to take some employment to support themselves during their study. All students who have obtained a baccalaureate can enter a university and there is no selection procedure or *numerus fixus* for psychology students.

The membership of the French Society of Psychology is comparatively small. In 1977 there were about 1500 members. Some 27% of these are work psychologists (de Montmollin, 1978). However many of these work psychologists are engaged in a limited and traditional type of activity, e.g. selection, working frequently as consultants. Research interests are restricted by lack of funding, except in the sphere of ergonomics, which shows signs of developing and provides more opportunities for work psychologists. Organizational psychology is much less developed, with French industrial sociologists showing a livelier interest in the study of organizations than psychologists.

South Europe: Some figures for Italy (population 57 million) were provided by a survey carried out in 1975 by the Italian Psychological Society. This survey covered 965 psychologists, both members and non-members of the Society, 206 of whom identified themselves with work psychology. Spaltro (oral communication) points out that this is only a guide to the number in this field, and almost certainly excludes psychologists working in industry who, for a variety of reasons, do not wish to be known by the title of psychologist. As in France, there is an enormous number of students who embark at the study of psychology (estimated at some 20 000 students in 1978) but with a correspondingly high dropout. Only about 700 graduate each year. Psychology is known to be taught and practised on a small scale in Spain and Portugal, but information on these countries is difficult to obtain.

South East Europe: Here again data are very scanty. It is known that there are some professional work psychologists in the Balkan countries. An account of the situation in Yugoslavia was given by Professor Boris Petz from Zagreb University in a conference paper. He states that probably no one knows exactly how many work psychologists there are in this country, although estimates have been given of 150–200. It seems that employment opportunities for such psychologists are limited. In a paper by Seminara (1976) describing a visit to Bulgaria

in 1974, it is pointed out that the Bulgarian Psychological Association
was then only 5 years old and had between 200 and 250 members,
comprising almost all Bulgarian psychologists at the time. At that date
there was no one with a doctoral degree in psychology and university
training programmes were of recent origin, e.g. in 1974 a department
of psychology was formed at the University of Sofia.

Eastern Europe: The socio-political situation in Eastern European
countries has had a considerable influence on the development of
psychology. In the years 1945-9 there was a rapid growth of
psychological institutes and many university chairs were established,
based on pre-war traditions. However, it was not until the late nineteen
fifties and early sixties that contacts were established with the West —
resulting in the translation of American and other studies for the
benefit of the growing population of psychologists. Poland provides
one of the most interesting examples of the development of work
psychology in Eastern Europe, an account of which is given by
Dobrzyński, in Section 2. Here it is sufficient to note that figures
supplied by the Ministry of Labour and Social Welfare for 1978 list
2703 people holding a master's degree in psychology (population of
Poland is 35 million), of whom 516 had specialized in industrial
psychology. In all, 554 psychologists, having obtained a degree, were
not employed in this profession, while 534 were working as industrial
psychologists, although only 60% of these had a degree in industrial
psychology and some 10% were clinical psychologists. For Czecho-
slovakia it was estimated that there are about 300 work psychologists
(total population 15 million) and there were about 200 in the German
Democratic Republic (population 17 million) in 1975. We have been
unable to obtain any statistics for the Soviet Union, but there is one
estimate, based on conference attendance, which puts the figure for
work psychologists in 1975 at between 700 and 900.

It is of interest to compare these figures with those from the United
States. Figure 2, which is taken from the "American Psychologist",
(McKinney, 1976) shows the growth curve for the membership of APA.
At the present time about 7% of the members of APA belong to the
I/O and engineering psychology divisions, compared to 37% in the
clinical psychology division.

Comparing Figs 1 and 2 it can be seen that the upturn of the curve
in the US begins in the nineteen thirties, whereas in Holland this is in

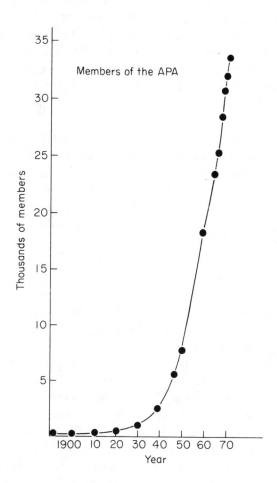

FIG. 2 Membership of the American Psychological Association.

the nineteen sixties. Psychological expansion in the US clearly occurred much earlier. This applies not just to the comparison with Holland, but is true throughout Europe, although in the case of the United Kingdom the gap is somewhat smaller.

The picture emerging from all these data is that, whereas in the south and south east of Europe, psychology as a whole is at the early

stages of its growth, in the north and west it can be regarded as firmly
established. Eastern Europe takes a position somewhere between these
two. The very large number of students seeking to study the subject
indicates a high level of sustained interest. But work psychology is
certainly not the first preference of these students, of whom the great
majority aspire to practise as clinical psychologists. Nevertheless, it
should be noted that work psychology, particularly in Sweden,
Germany and Holland, offers identifiable job opportunities over a
broad area.

From the numbers it can also be inferred that in many countries
work psychologists have achieved a kind of "critical mass", or are likely
to do so in the next few years. This might not be apparent from the
professional literature. We are therefore now discussing a situation
differing from the one obtaining a decade or so ago when there were
only limited numbers of psychologists employed in this field.

D.   American influence

A major consequence of the earlier development of psychology in the
United States is that the subject in Europe has been considerably
influenced by American work.

Teaching and research programmes have been based to a large
extent on the American literature. Since World War II many
Europeans have undertaken graduate studies in the US and have made
extended study visits. In addition, many American work psychologists
have been invited as guest lecturers and/or research fellows to
European institutes. This has been facilitated by the growth of
management and business education, based on the model of American
business schools in many cases, resulting in some European
foundations seeking to recruit American staff. A considerable number
of undergraduate textbooks, as well as more specialized publications
used in Europe, originated in the United States and American journals
are widely read. English is the second language in most European
universities. Publications by European work psychologists usually cite
numerous American references, so it is easy for students to get the
impression that the most interesting research in work psychology is
being undertaken in the USA.

Now that work psychology in Europe has emerged as a critical mass in its own right there is developing awareness, on both sides of the Atlantic, that significant advances are being made in Europe as well as America. Students are no longer content to base their studies on American textbooks, most of which make no reference to authors outside the United States, and press for texts more closely related to their own culture. Thus, although American influence is still strong, the balance is changing in some instances towards a more European based psychology of work.

E.   Professional roles of work psychologists

Over the years there have been marked changes in the professional roles adopted by work psychologists. In its early days the subject was seen in terms of scientific applications, entailing psychologists working solely as scientific researchers. The implicit model was that of taking an established body of knowledge, developed largely through laboratory experimentation, and applying it to specific issues in the sphere of work. At that time, there was no question of work psychologists themselves influencing policies or being involved in implementing any action arising from their findings.

During both World Wars, work psychologists were challenged to deal with some specific problems — e.g. in the First World War, advances in appraisal and selection procedures were made in the placement of men drafted to the US army while, in Britain, research on fatigue amongst munition workers foreshadowed the establishment of industrial psychology. In the Second World War, besides extensive progress being made in selection for new tasks, e.g. aircrew, principles of group dynamics were systematically applied, both diagnostically and therapeutically. The latter developments derived largely from the work of Kurt Lewin, a refugee from Nazi Germany, who went to the United States in the nineteen thirties and who exerted a profound influence on social and applied psychology.

After the Second World War, a new style of research emerged of which an early example was the work of Elliot Jaques (1952) in the Glacier Metal Company, described in his book "The Changing Culture of a Factory". The essence of this approach — usually designated action research — is the involvement of the researcher with the client in a joint commitment to a course of action. This entails work psychologists abandoning the position of detached expert and sharing responsibility with the client for the outcome and implementation of the research strategy. Most of the Scandinavian projects on work organization and job design, as well as industrial democracy experiments, have been carried out on this basis (cf. Emery and Thorsrud, 1969; Thorsrud, 1972; Elden, 1979). Even in the more traditional spheres of vocational guidance and selection there has been a change of emphasis over the last fifteen years from concern with prediction to a concentration on process (e.g. career development, management development).

Such interventionist approaches, whereby researchers seek to influence behaviour rather than merely to describe and record it, are not confined to work psychologists but have also been adopted by other applied social scientists. However, the involvement of work psychologists in programmes of planned organizational change (Bennis, Benne and Chin, 1964) and similar interventions has furthered the diversification of their professional roles and activities, e.g. as consultants, trainers, process analysts, and so on. In these roles, a prerequisite for the task is the development of a trust relationship between the work psychologist and the members of the client organization.

Whatever their mode of operation, work psychologists have always shown an "inner directedness" (cf. Riesman, 1950), i.e. they tend to be preoccupied with the technical capabilities of their discipline and look primarily to each other for approval and validation of their work. However, in the late sixties and early seventies, younger psychologists began to look beyond their immediate reference group and became concerned with the wider social issues and the relevance of their subject to the well-being of society. At the same time, philosophers of science were challenging the supremacy of the positivistic scientific approach and this led to a more critical stance towards psychology in general and to work psychology in particular. This meant that even the clearly defined role of the research worker became subject to review and reappraisal. For example, some now seriously question the assumptions of independence and absence of bias implicit in this role.

F.   Continuity and identity

Psychologists identify themselves with their chosen subject so that an important element in their self-image is that of practising as a psychologist. In other words, they see themselves as members of a professional group, with whom they share values about how they should behave. In dealing with clients, they expect to act, not as individuals, but as representatives of their profession, from which they look for guidance as to what they can and should be expected to do as practitioners. Many of these shared standards and values are implicit, and are acquired through close association with members and colleagues, rather than through any formal induction, although most professional psychological associations have a code of ethics. These informal arrangements serve both as a form of quality control and of socialization, whereby individuals learn to adopt a specific stance towards clients and members of other professions. Thus, for work psychologists, as for any other profession, fellow members constitute the most important reference group. Several examples, both of the supporting and the controlling aspects of their peers on the activities of work psychologists, will be found later in this book, but here we would like to emphasize three points.

1. Without such support the practitioner is vulnerable in situations of conflicting loyalty and group interest, e.g. it might be difficult for some psychologists to defend the right of both applicants and prospective employers to obtain the results of psychological testing, if they could not refer to the code of practice and ethical standards expected of them as members of the profession.
2. The peer group provides the role models for effective professional behaviour. These are distinct from the scientific models to which psychologists are exposed as students. For example, the social skills and negotiating skills, as well as the ability to start and terminate relationships with clients on a note of an enhanced mutual respect, are difficult to acquire without some form of apprenticeship to an experienced practitioner. Even later there are occasions when con-sultation with professional colleagues is needed, especially when dealing with situations not previously encountered.
3. The peer group provides for the updating of practical knowledge, exchange of information, and it acts as a sounding board for the discussions of difficulties associated with work in a complex field.

Unlike some of the long-established professions, such as law and medicine, which have well-regulated institutional procedures leading ultimately to a professional licence to practice, work psychology lacks such structures. University training programmes in psychology are directed towards producing scientists rather than practitioners. As a number of applied psychologists have pointed out (e.g. Varela, 1975; Davidson, 1977), training for professional work needs to be different from that aimed at pure research, particularly at the more advanced stages. At the moment it is very much a matter of chance where the young graduates embarking on professional work will receive appropriate guidance and practice in handling the variety of situations which they will confront as work psychologists. Not only are there no formal training schemes of supervised professional practice, but also there is much ambiguity about what level of responsibility should be placed upon a new graduate entering the field. Notwithstanding the absence of systematic professional socialization, work psychologists nevertheless do hold certain values in common. For example they feel that their training puts them in a superior position to laymen in investigating problems, and also that they are better qualified to deal with certain social problems. The majority would be unhappy to be mistaken for members of other professional groups either by clients or the public at large.

An important function of a professional association is to preserve the identity of the domain and to ensure continuity from one generation to the next. Consequently these bodies are inclined to be conservative in outlook, seeing their task as primarily that of preserving an achieved position rather than extending it. Their definitions of rules and criteria of membership are inevitably related to the situation or conditions appertaining at a given point in time and so they are not geared to take account of change.

Given the changing circumstances in which work psychologists have been and are being required to operate, with the associated diversity of roles to which we have already referred, the profession as a whole is slow to adapt to these new activities. One result of this is that work psychologists functioning in the newer areas not only experience role ambiguity but cannot count on the support of the professional association in the same way as those concerned with more traditional activities. Thus, whereas work psychologists doing selection and research are clearly recognizable as members of the profession, those engaged in interventionist approaches, such as organizational development, may be regarded as fringe members. In the latter instance, a further complication is that non-psychologists also work in these areas, and therefore the nature of his or her activities is not, in itself, sufficient to identify the practitioner as a work psychologist. The relationship between the individual and the professional reference group can be very tenuous in these new areas of activity. It may be described more as a situation of mutual coexistence than as the profession supporting and exerting control over the individual, and the extent to which they subscribe to shared values is rather obscure. There seems to be a range of tolerance beyond which the individual work psychologist operating at the margins of the domain may feel it is more appropriate to identify with another reference group, e.g. management consultants, in which case the psychological profession ceases to be of major significance for the person concerned. These trends suggest that the profession of work psychology is confronted by at least two problems: how to accommodate to changes in the task environment, and how to preserve its identity in the face of an increasing diversity of membership. It is almost a truism that we are living in a period of rapid social, technological and political change, which create what Emery and Trist (1965) call a "turbulent environment".

No less than any other group, work psychologists are exposed to this turbulent environment, which means that the knowledge and skills acquired during their initial training have to be applied under very different operating conditions. Also that they frequently find themselves having to work with and for others who do not share their values, and who expect them to provide ready solutions to very complex problems.

Furthermore, young psychologists entering the profession tend to have a different outlook and ideology from the more established members which leads them to question the relevance of many traditional activities and views. The profession therefore has somehow to adapt itself to pressures for change arising from within and without. To date, such accommodation has only been attempted on an *ad hoc* basis.

Another dimension of change within the profession is the rapid development of psychological technology. Psychologists have always been ingenious in constructing techniques of measurement, assessment, data analysis and of behaviour modification. This inventiveness now includes strategies for organizational change, which have

provided work psychologists with new opportunities and increased the
potential range of application. It has also posed new problems,
e.g. many people are frightened by the prospect of techniques which
claim to alter human behaviour, seeing these as threats to individual
liberty. They may therefore resist any attempts to apply psychology in
their sphere of work.

It is very difficult, given the present structure of professional bodies,
most of which originated as learned scientific societies, to foresee
anything but slow accommodation to these changes. Their structures
are not geared to professional socialization and adaptation, but to the
training and qualifications of psychologists in general and to the
exchange of scientific information. Although the problems we have
mentioned are shared to some extent with other branches of applied
psychology, e.g. clinical and educational psychology, they are more
acute in the case of work psychologists, because the latter embraces far
more diverse activities and roles than the others.

Psychological associations have always sought to impose fairly rigid
entrance qualifications on their members, but they have been largely
unable to exercise oversight or control over their practitioners working
in the field. Although in some countries there is, at best, a procedure
for dealing with complaints from clients, and for excluding individuals
from the profession as a consequence of serious misbehaviour, the
more common situation is lack of definition as to what constitutes
malpractice. It is also left to the individual to decide whether or not to
accept assignments which lie outside his or her normal area of
competence.

What strikes us most in looking at these professional issues is that, in
comparison with the institutional arrangements for the discussion of
scientific matters, those for discussion of professional affairs are only
rudimentary.

Conventions are almost exclusively held for the discussion of
scientific affairs at either national or international level, although
there may be occasional papers on professional issues. Likewise the
many journals on the subject of work psychology publish articles which
are almost exclusively scientific in content. In our opinion this is a
serious deficiency, particularly in view of the large number of students
reading psychology and those likely to enter the profession of work
psychology in the near future.

Unless opportunities are created for mutual discussion between practitioners and scientists and older and younger members of the profession concerning these problems, there may be a serious threat to the identity of the profession as a whole and an associated risk of fragmentation.

There are a few instances where such discussions have been started. One is the setting up of a newly formulated code of ethics for the Dutch Psychological Association which was drafted by a group of university psychologists and practitioners, and which was widely discussed before it was accepted in 1975 (NIP, 1975). The division of work psychologists formulated a set of additional rules which was also widely discussed. Part of these discussions have been published by the journal of the association, *De Psycholoog*, which has increasingly devoted space to papers dealing with professional issues.

The emotional consequences of having to cope with change, whether as an individual or as a member of a professional association, should not be underestimated. Role conflict, role ambiguity and future uncertainty are well-known stressors leading to anxiety and doubts about the value of individual contributions (van Vucht Tijssen *et al.*, 1978). The immaturity of work psychology as a profession means that there are insufficiently clear guidelines for practitioners as to how to cope with these problems.

As Hoch (1962) stated of psychology as a whole in the United States almost twenty years ago: "Conference after conference finds the profession asking itself broad yet pointed questions. Where is the field moving? What can be done to steer its course? If, indeed, this is possible, in which direction ought the psychology of tomorrow be channelled? Should the profession hold the line until the complexion of the field clears up?" These sentiments are particularly apt when applied to the psychology of work in Europe today. They reflect the uncertainties which are the inevitable accompaniments of growth and change, especially those resulting from the turbulence of the political and social environments of the later nineteen sixties and nineteen seventies.

G. Whither the profession?

A basic question for any profession is what is a desirable future, and how this may be obtained. This is a matter of survival and of maintaining the continuity and identity which we have mentioned earlier. It is not a question about Utopia or an ideal state, but one of working for realistic goals which reconcile the expectations and needs of members of the profession and of the wider society of which they are a part. The issue can be broken down to three main questions: What services should psychologists render, i.e. what business are they in? On whose behalf should they be working — whose servant are they? And the third one: In what way should psychology be organized professionally to render these services?

These are the questions to which the further chapters of this book are addressed. Chapter 2 deals with the development of the domain of work psychology, with particular reference to the changing nature of the profession, and some consequences for future activities. Following this, the issues of legitimation and conflicting values are discussed in Chapter 3.

2 The Development of the Domain

A.   What is a domain?

The concept of a domain is associated particularly with Thompson (1967) who argues that any organized collectivity of people must decide what is their purpose or mission, first in terms of goods produced or services rendered and, second, the client group or groups for whom these goods or services are provided. Thompson, in writing this, was referring to organizations in general, but his conception applies equally to professions, considered as occupational groupings and not just as professional bodies. In other words, those who identify with the title of work psychologist, regardless of whether they are members of a formal professional association, share a domain with others, the boundaries of which they help to define by their own activities. Therefore professions may be analysed from an open systems perspective, in the same way as Thompson analysed other organizations.

A particular characteristic of domains in this context is that they are subject to constant change as a result of the interaction of members of the profession with their task environment. The shape of the territory is always changing; furthermore it is guarded by the occupants in terms of their rights to practise their profession to the exclusion of rival claimants. Furthermore, Thompson suggests that strategies can be developed for the management and extension of the domain on a systematic basis, with particular reference to dependencies on the task environment. This means that work psychologists or indeed members

21

of any other profession, are actively responsible for the domain in which they operate, and are not simply passive providers of services to clients. The domain of the psychology of work has undergone tremendous changes in the last twenty years. Whereas, in the early nineteen fifties, it was relatively restricted, with most professionals in the area engaged in selection, the field is now so wide and differentiated that it is impossible for a single practitioner to encompass the subject. For example, on the first page of the large *Handbook of Industrial and Organizational Psychology*, edited by Dunnette (1976), he states: "Industrial and organizational psychology's scope is so broad and so diverse that I have been frustrated in my efforts to develop a conceptionally satisfying or dimensionally clear structure." Dunnette's handbook includes contributions from 43 authors, covering 37 topics ranging from such traditional topics as personnel training to such newer areas as conflict and conflict management, organizational structure and climate, and stress and behaviour in organizations. And even then he lists four potential areas of concern which he has excluded.

A key to this growth and diversification is provided by the addition of the word "organizational" to "industrial" to describe the area of work psychology. Members of several disciplines were drawn to the study of organizations in the nineteen fifties and sixties, e.g. industrial sociologists, economists, systems theorists, with the result that theories of organizations have developed which draw on concepts from a number of fields.

After the Second World War, work psychologists found that they had to extend their focus, not only from the individual to the small group, but also to the organization and the wider environment, and in so doing had to take account of the concepts and approaches of other disciplines. It is interesting to note that in sociology the reverse process occurred, in that sociologists became aware of individual perceptions and their influence upon organizational processes. In consequence, the field of organizational studies is part of the domain of practitioners from many disciplines with considerable overlap between them.

Although work psychology has become established in different countries at rather different rates, as we showed in Chapter 1, the pattern of development of employment opportunities has been broadly similar. Originally work psychologists were employed almost entirely in universities and/or research institutions. The field was small, and most members of the profession knew one another.

As a result of approaches from clients and government agencies for help with specific application problems, work psychologists became employed outside laboratories and academic settings. Thus, although their involvement in the applied field was initially in response to requests from outside, they became more aware of the new opportunities presented and more pro-active in their applied work. A reciprocal effect was a growth in employment opportunities particularly in academic teaching appointments. The best documentated example is for the Netherlands. Table 1 shows the relevant figures taken from Krijnen (1975).

TABLE 1
Employment of work psychologists in the Netherlands

	Industry %	University %
1963	28	14
1972	16	28

In absolute terms, the number of man years of employment for work psychologists working in industry in 1963, 1966, 1969 and 1972 were, respectively, 54, 63, 74, and 124. The corresponding figure for the growth of psychological subfaculties within the universities were 49, 84, 157 and 290. Although the latter comprises all psychologists in teaching posts and not only work psychologists, it should be noted that the rate of growth in the universities is more than double that of employment within industry. Furthermore, the figures do not include technical universities and schools of economics which have a number of work psychologists on their teaching staff. Drenth (1978) has reported that the man years represented by faculty staff in work psychology were 19·9 in 1965/1966, but increased to 76·6 in 1977.

In the next decade it seems to us that yet another pattern will emerge. After the great expansion of universities throughout Europe in the nineteen sixties, the seventies have seen a period of little growth and of projected cutback in university expenditures. Therefore work psychologists who aspire to academic posts are now faced with very limited opportunities in this sphere. Conversely, the range of jobs which may be designated broadly as "applied social science" has increased and is still increasing. Provided that work psychologists are prepared to compete with graduates from other disciplines and to engage in activities requested by clients, to which they feel they can make an appropriate contribution, in our view the future employment of work psychologists in the secondary and tertiary sector may be viewed optimistically. In this connection it may be noted that this accords with the projection made by Krijnen (1976).

To date, much of the development of the domain of work psychology has occurred on a rather haphazard basis, together with opportunism on the part of some practitioners. The overlapping interests with other disciplines, resulting in a decline in opportunities solely restricted to psychologists, suggests that professionals should take stock of these developments and decide what to do about them. The logic of the argument that members of a profession are instrumental in shaping their own domain suggests that the time has come for a more systematic approach to these issues.

This is easier to advocate than to implement. Given the tendency on the part of individuals, professional organizations and clients to seek short-term solutions to problems, the pressure is always to concentrate on immediate issues. What we are suggesting is that, probably without realizing it, work psychologists who operate in this mode are letting others shape the domain for them, rather than taking responsibility for this themselves. Whereas it may be too much to ask the individual practitioner, concerned with his own bread and butter, to think in terms of ten years ahead, we suggest that the formal professional bodies might well put this on their agendas. Some steps in this direction have already been taken, e.g. by the APA division 14 (Campbell *et al.*, 1976) in setting up a long-range planning committee, although this model might not be the most suited to other countries. Admittedly, skill in analysing future needs is still very rudimentary because of the tendency to base most forecasts on extrapolations of the situation in the past. Nevertheless, in our view this is no excuse for not attempting the exercise. Otherwise we run the risk of *ad hoc* growth and possible fragmentation of what is already a very complex domain. Let us state our own assumptions about the future.

1. Growth and diversification of the domain will continue. Psychologists are already employed in a far greater variety of positions than formerly, and the employment trends suggest that this phenomenon will continue. How this will affect the domain is

difficult to predict because much depends on the nature of the tasks, the practitioners' expectations of support from the profession, the extent to which these are fulfilled and the competing claims of other reference groups.

2. It seems that proportionally more work psychologists will be employed outside academic settings and that they will seek to define the domain differently from their more scientifically oriented colleagues.

3. It follows from (2) that there will be increasing tension between practitioners and scientists, as each group seeks to become the dominant faction controlling the shape of the domain.

4. Unless these tensions can be managed in a way which is satisfactory to both groups, the likelihood of splinter groups forming and/or work psychologists ceasing to identify with the profession itself but adhering to other reference groups is a very real one.

5. We cannot assume that work psychology will necessarily remain in the domain of psychology as a whole, at least in some countries. Already many work psychologists teach in business or management schools rather than in university psychology departments and work psychology is often optional, rather than a compulsory part of university training programmes.

B.   The diversification of employment

At the present time, newly graduated work psychologists take up jobs when and where they are available. Many of these, as we have already indicated, are not designated specifically for psychologists, or indeed for social scientists, but consist of various administrative, managerial or service-type positions. In these situations, the psychology graduate's activities are determined to a considerable extent by the employer's and/or client's needs, but nevertheless they may offer opportunities for extending the area of professional competence. Much depends on the psychologist's own reference groups, on immediate colleagues, and the degree of support expected and received from the profession as a whole as to whether the frontier of the domain is pushed forward or shrinks in these circumstances.

This may be illustrated by reference to two areas in which a substantial number of work psychologists are employed, namely market research and organizational development. In both these areas, work psychologists quite frequently prefer to be involved with their formal or informal associations of fellow practitioners, than to seek colleagueship through the professional bodies. If, as a result, they cease to identify with fellow psychologists they may become lost to the profession.

Market research is an example in this respect. Whereas, in the nineteen sixties, it was considered as a legitimate subsection of work psychology in a number of countries, by the end of the seventies it has become a largely separate activity. In the case of organizational development, although academics discuss the theoretical foundations of these types of interventions, they would regard the bulk of practitioners as lacking sufficient academic qualifications in psychology to consider them as legitimate members of the psychological profession. However, to the individual psychologist newly arriving in this field, and working as a practitioner, it is more important that he allies himself with those having practical experience than that he seeks his reference group in academic institutions.

Although psychologists study the reference groups of others, insufficient attention has been paid to their own, particularly in the area of work psychology. The transition from an academic environment in which common values can be assumed, and a scientific approach is taken for granted, to an environment in which short-term problem solving and expediency predominate, can be traumatic for the young graduate. He or she is confronted with the need to establish credibility with fellow employees who, themselves, belong to different task and interest groups and who have little or no idea what to expect of a psychologist. The situation of course will differ according to whether or not other psychologists are employed in the same organization but, in many cases, there will be no other people trained in the discipline in the immediate environment. There seems little doubt that, in the latter case, an individual will experience conflict as to how far to join the groups represented by his or her colleagues, and how far to retain or signal his or her identity as a psychologist.

Closely associated with this dilemma is the tension between the scientific and the practitioner approach, to which we have already referred. Except in academic institutions, the primary task of work psychologists is seen not as the extension of knowledge but as action or intervention in the solution of problems, whether at an individual, group or organizational level. Even among academic work psychologists, however, there is disagreement as to the "state of the art" concerning application, some stressing that the way forward must lie through traditional research approaches, whereas others favour learning through collaborative action with client systems and willingness to enter relatively uncharted areas.

This conflict is even more marked in the relationship between theoretical psychology and work psychology. Some theoretical psychologists like to emphasize that knowledge in the subject as a whole is too limited to permit direct application, except in a very few instances. They therefore regard practitioners' claims that they can help clients as both exaggerated and unwarranted. For example, Duijker (1977) writing as a social psychologist, warns practitioners to be very cautious in making prescriptions on the basis of a science which can only be descriptive. When so many issues are still unresolved it is rather presumptuous to tell others how they should solve their problems. Since application always entails values, Duijker doubts whether a psychologist can claim any superiority over informed laymen in solving practical problems.

On the other hand, legitimation of the practitioner's activities comes from clients who, in continuing to ask for services, imply that they find the practitioner's contributions valuable. Furthermore, work psychologists' expertise in certain areas, e.g. selection, is more appropriate than that of any other professional group. In terms of the domain, the tug-of-war between the perspective represented by the advancement of knowledge versus that of application of knowledge precludes any static or long-term definition.

C.   Content of the domain

Although we have indicated that practitioners themselves bear a responsibility for shaping their domain, there is no doubt that societal needs, as expressed through requests for help from a variety of clients, are extremely influential.

Client needs inevitably change over the course of time but, since the end of the Second World War, the rate of technological, economic, political and social change has presented clients with unfamiliar problems and choices which they have not encountered previously.

For example, the advent of electronic data processing has had an enormous impact on clerical work, and the prospect of complete automation of industrial processes presents a challenge to current employment policies. In these circumstances, which can be very stressful to the individuals concerned, help is often sought from work psychologists and others, whose experience is judged to be relevant to the problem. Some of the problems posed to them are not necessarily amenable to psychological approaches but, nevertheless, work psychologists may feel that it is imperative for their credibility that they attempt to deal with them. In such instances the desire to meet the needs of clients acts as a formative influence on the shape of the domain. Consequently, work psychologists are involved in dealing with all kinds of new issues arising from the turbulent environment. These, however, have not been documented in any systematic fashion and professional training is still orientated towards the more limited range of services and technical assistance which psychologists provided some twenty years ago.

One attempt to explore the nature of client needs, especially to find out in which sense these might contribute to new employment opportunities, was made by Krijnen (1976). He interviewed a sample of key people who could be expected to be well informed about future trends. The study dealt with all psychologists; but for work psychologists he found that it was expected that there would be job opportunities related to: career guidance, recurrent education, participation programmes, organizational problems, work stress and communication problems. In other cases, it is work psychologists themselves who take the initiative, whether employed within or outside organizations. They see their function as that of maintaining or extending their area of operation, especially in the face of rival practitioners, and seek to persuade clients to give them an opportunity to exercise their skills.

Thus developments are of two broad kinds. On the one hand we see the establishment of new types of services to meet particular needs, and on the other the growing awareness by scientists of the potentialities of new areas of research. For example, a consultancy firm may develop a reputation for expertise in dealing with particular kinds of problems such as the effects of automation, health service organizational structures, or job evaluation and reward systems, which stimulate clients to come forward with new questions and other consultants and researchers to look at these issues. But initiatives also come from the academic world, where opinion leaders can be identified who, through publications, invited lectures and the development of their research programmes, try to influence their fellows as to the main issues to be tackled. Examples can be seen in papers from Heller (1976), Davidson (1977) and de Wolff (1977), of attempts to direct the development of the domain in a certain direction and others will be found in Section 2. Through these processes a whole array of possibilities is constantly presented, some of which become reinforced and others extinguished. This occurs through the reciprocal process of interaction between clients and psychologists, as well as between work psychologists themselves who interact with one another through a number of networks. It is in this way that the domain is shaped.

Many of these issues are picked up on an individual basis, i.e. through individuals responding to approaches from others. However, for any topic to achieve prominence as an area of sustained endeavour, there must be activities on a sufficient scale to carry it beyond what is possible at the individual level. This is not a question simply of the number of psychologists involved but also of time scale. Many topics require concentrated effort over a number of years by teams of people, rather than individual investigators. This is particularly true of the complex problems which now confront us but, it should be noted, the profession of work psychology is not well adapted to deal with them in a systematic way. We have the impression that almost too much is attempted by too few, leading to a dilution of effectiveness. Problems like alienation, absenteeism, unemployment, stress, continuous education, quality of working life, etc. seem to call for large-scale research efforts. In many countries the existing arrangements for the funding and conducting of research do not permit the large-scale longitudinal type of work which is really needed (cf. Pugh *et al.*, 1975; Barry *et al.*, 1978). In this respect we may be paying a price for diversity. This contrasts with the past when the concentrated attack on problems of selection was made possible by the restriction of the field and the willingness of powerful clients to underwrite research in this area.

Given that the present resources are inadequate to meet the range of potential problems which might be of relevance to work psychologists, a case can be made for market research to identify more clearly what are the present and future needs of prospective clients and society as a whole. And also to investigate the distribution of skills and interests within the profession. This would need to take into account not only present potential, but also what work psychologists could offer in the future if training programmes were revised and extended. Associated with both the above exercises it is desirable to evaluate the expertise offered by other groups, who may compete with work psychologists, and the likely extent of this competition. Nor should it be assumed that the relationship will necessarily be one of competition, but the possibility of collaboration with other professions to render a more effective service to clients should be explored.

Present trends also point to a change of direction in the main activities of work psychologists in terms of the scientist–practitioner dimension. Although the prevailing emphasis in training programmes is still on study and the search for understanding human behaviour in organizations, what employers and clients now expect are interventionist approaches. An important influence here has been the growing appreciation that scientific investigations do not solve organizational problems, although they may, hopefully, provide the basis of more informed decisions. The stock of knowledge used by most practitioners in assisting others to deal with change is a very pragmatic one, based on experience and the testing out of ideas in interaction with clients, rather than on scientific reports. If this is to be the prevailing mode of activity in the future then training programmes are likely to be much more experiential in their content. Signs of this are already evident in the growth of fieldwork projects, social skill training and experience-based learning exercises in several programmes.

D.   Preservation of the domain

The need for market research ties up with the question of the preservation of the domain. In defining a domain a basic assumption is that there is an underlying unity of purpose and shared values. However, now that the field has become so broad and diverse in character and looks like continuing to remain so, this assumed unity should perhaps be questioned. We referred above to the risk of fragmentation associated with the emergence of specialized subgroups, especially when these are closely related to other disciplines. These subgroups are sometimes recognized by the professional bodies in the form of sections or divisions devoted to different branches of psychology — but in this context work psychology is usually regarded as if it were a unified area. As we have shown in the case of marketing researchers and O.D. practitioners, there are areas of work psychology whose practitioners may well break away from the main professional body. The more specialized groups which emerge, the greater is the problem of preserving a common definition for the domain as a whole.

We still do not know sufficiently well what determines the attachment to and identification of members with one domain rather than another, although some clues are provided by the functions of professional associations. These serve to regulate and control entry to the profession, codes of conduct, and symbolize the public image of their members. To the latter, however, they are also a source of guidance and support, although this is not necessarily a declared aim in their charter and statutes.

Members both individually and collectively have expectations of the kind of support they expect to receive and of the rewards of membership. Work psychologists operating at the margins of the profession may well find themselves in situations in which a professional body from another domain appears to offer greater benefits than that to which they currently belong. It is these groups who formally or informally identify with others who pose a threat to the unity of the domain. One cannot assume that different work psychologists in these boundary positions will see the situation uniformly. In other words one can find some ergonomists who prefer to belong to an ergonomic society, whereas others identify more with psychology.

The situation is complicated by the fact that work psychology has no generalist–specialist structure as pertains in the domain of medicine. Whereas specialist advice in medicine can usually only be obtained through referral by a general practitioner, in work psychology there is no such arrangement. Not only is there no clearly defined role of a general practitioner, but also there are few areas of specialization requiring formal qualifications and a licence to practise. Most work psychologists will concede that they cannot cover the whole domain. The absence of a specialist structure is perhaps one of the factors which increases the risks of losing territory. We do not suggest that the medical model is necessarily the most appropriate for work psychology, but it would seem that some deliberate attempt at structuring the specialist subgroups in a way which links them with the whole of the domain is needed.

This may require experiments with a number of structures before an adequate solution can be found because the *ad hoc* growth of the field has made it so complex. It may also mean that the structure which becomes established in one country will not apply readily in another where the domain is at a different stage of development or moves in a different direction.

E. The dominant faction

Mok's (1973) contention that, in any profession, there are always a number of competing definitions of the domain is particularly true of the psychology of work. Seen from the perspective of a specialist group, the domain appears to have certain attitudes which are not perceived or which are regarded as of little relevance by those in another faction. This is clearly illustrated by the content and editorial policies of a number of journals which can be categorized as belonging to the domain. There are specialist journals catering for ergonomics, psychology and management, organizational development, industrial relations and applied experimental psychology, to name but some. Both authors and editors have clear ideas as to the appropriateness of contributions within each of these sub-domains. At the same time, they do not claim to be able to evaluate work in other sub-areas from an equally informed standpoint. Nevertheless, they do not dispute the right of these other sub-areas to be included within the total domain of work psychology.

An entirely different situation obtains, however, if a specialist sub-area is perceived by the others as making a bid to control the domain as a whole. In these circumstances tension, rivalry and competition to achieve a dominant position of influence become apparent, a solution which may reinforce the tendency toward fragmentation mentioned earlier. Conversely, if the domain as a whole appears to be threatened by territorial claims from another discipline, the various factions may combine in defence of what they regard as a shared definition. Binding influences in these circumstances can be traced to common basic training, shared values of the importance of research, implicit assumptions about professional ethics, and mutual respect for achievements in different areas. When the divergent areas combine in this way, a strong force is created, which pulls the domain together and masks some of the differences. This may be contrasted with the situation where, in the absence of any external threat or group-dividing influences, there is a tendency for the field to fragment.

The above description forms the background to the contest from which a dominant faction can emerge at any point. This faction can be identified by the overriding influence on policy and practice within the domain, e.g. relating to criteria governing professional appointments, editorships of journals, nomination of work psychologists to serve on government or other committees, and such similar positions. The members of the dominant faction will also be found in key parts of formal professional bodies and as informal gatekeepers in a variety of academic and consultancy activities. Closely associated with these functions is an influence on allocation of rewards available to the members of the profession although, in this, as in other respects, control can never be complete. Political lobbies and other groups in the environment are also important.

It should be noted that, for the reasons outlined above, the dominant faction changes with circumstances and over time. There are always forces at work seeking to topple the present faction in favour of another, and of equally strong forces striving to maintain the *status quo*. In practice, these tensions epitomize the problems of continuity, identity and adaptation to change which can be observed in all social groupings at the present time. Thus, although we have discerned a move towards a pragmatic interventionist type of work psychology and some reflection of the implications of this within current training programmes, nevertheless the predominance of positivistic social science is still clearly evident. To a great extent this is due to the dominant faction in psychology as a whole which holds ambivalent views about the legitimacy of work psychology within the overall domain. Consequently, there are tensions between the two. Some marked differences exist in this respect between European countries, e.g. work psychology is generally well regarded in the Netherlands, but, with the exception of ergonomics, is considered of minor importance in France. In Britain occupational psychology struggles to avoid coming at the bottom of the pecking order.

It may be noted that members of the dominant faction are usually preoccupied with short-term objectives and are therefore relatively unaware of their present actions in shaping the future. If the market research approach advocated in the last section is to be undertaken it is clearly desirable that they not only participate in this, but seek actively to implement the findings. In other words it is amongst these people that we would hope to see responsible action in collaborative activities in long-term planning. We stress the word collaborative here since it seems to us that, in most countries, there is relatively little interaction between the members of the dominant faction on such matters. This is because the professional aspects of their activities tend to be taken for granted and are not discussed systematically in the same way as the scientific content of the domain, which forms the subject of conferences, seminars and informal discussions.

The need for some structured method and arrangements for discussing problems and strategies in the profession became increasingly evident in the preparation of the review article, published by Personnel Psychology (de Wolff and Shimmin, 1976), which we mentioned in the preface of this book. There we discovered that some real areas of concern to members of our group were professional and not scientific issues. Subsequent exchanges with American colleagues have shown that they endorse this view.

F.   Relationships with other disciplines

Another possible line of development which may be considered is that, rather than maintaining work psychology within the domain of psychology as a whole, it will become part of the larger domain of applied social science. Some strong arguments can be advanced for this line of development. For example, most of the newer sub-areas of work psychology like organizational behaviour draw on sociology and other disciplines as much as psychology. In addition, the subject is taught increasingly in the context of business schools and departments of applied social science rather than in traditional psychology departments. In the sphere of research, the problems presented invariably call for a multi-disciplinary approach, as do many consulting assignments. Therefore, work psychologists frequently find themselves alongside other social scientists and moving towards a common definition of an applied field. We have the impression that there is now a two-way flow of traffic between work psychology and other social sciences concerning concepts and methods.

While such convergence of approaches can and does occur in

applied work, it is another matter entirely to look for a fusion of two or more disciplines in the foreseeable future, given present educational and training systems. These are extremely influential in socializing students to identify with a particular discipline so that, by the time they enter employment, their self-image is that of a member of a disciplinary domain. Identities once formed are not easily changed. One of the obstacles in the way of effective mergers in that they are often seen as entailing a loss of identity by those involved. It takes considerable time for a new organization or institute to forge an identity of its own.

The arguments presented above suggest that many work psychologists will be caught in a form of approach — avoidance conflict about their identity and the domain to which they really belong. This is likely to induce oscillating responses, rather than a firm commitment to joining one or other professional group.

From a societal point of view the advantages of an integrated applied social science appear to outweigh those of the continued segregation of disciplines. Clients seeking advice do not discriminate between practitioners with regard to their basic training, but are only concerned to get a particular job done. In addition, as Krijnen's study showed (1975), there are comparatively few employment opportunities restricted to work psychologists. Therefore one must recognize the overlapping boundaries of different domains in the social sciences and the associated tensions of competing forces. As long as the dominant factions in the various disciplines reinforce present identities, the scenario presented here is likely to continue. But we must recognize that the turbulent environment in many countries could lead to discontinuity in developments and the emergence of entirely new structures.

G. The role of government

All the present indications are that in the next decade the domain will be subject to direct and indirect interventions by governments. This applies to all countries. This is a function of economic, social and political factors, which result in a scarcity of resources and changing expectations about the distribution of such resources as are available. For example, there is the question of whether educational provisions should concentrate on younger or older age groups, given the changing patterns of employment; and the measures taken to protect the rights of workers, including those designed to prevent discrimination against minority groups. Another example is the changing pattern of social insurance, linked with expectations that most people will not work for the whole of their adult life.

In recent years government policy has become a major source of influence shaping the domain in a number of ways.

1. There is the increasing legislation governing such matters as health and safety at work, employment practices, forms of industrial democracy, and other measures directly affecting employment relationships.
2. There is the role of government as a major employer of psychologists, either directly in its own departments and agencies, or indirectly through the funding of research programmes. Thus in Krijnen's study (1975) it was found that the income of some 70% of all psychologists was derived from government sources.
3. Most educational institutions in Europe are financed mainly by the state. This means that both the length of training programmes and the number of students entering them are subject to government control. In some countries this also affects formal recognition of the official title of psychologist.

In general, the profession of work psychology has not considered its relationship with government in any systematic way. Although there is tacit recognition of their financial dependence, like most professionals, work psychologists do not consider it gentlemanly (cf. Mok, 1973) to discuss this openly. Therefore, although members compete with one another to obtain research grants and government contracts they do not consider forming a combined lobby to promote their financial standing vis-á-vis other groups. Indeed, some members would view with dismay any attempt on the part of their professional associations to behave like a trade union. Likewise, very little is done in a combined fashion to promote members' intrinsic interests. They tend to assume that their views will be sought when appropriate, and do not attempt to monitor prospective legislation in terms of how it will affect their professional activities. The need to market the skills and expertise of work psychologists so that successive administrations are aware of, and appreciate what the profession has to offer, is not understood.

The relationship with government represents a main strand in the political dimension of the domain. This includes identifying the gatekeepers and those holding key positions in relevant networks. Although work psychologists are well aware of the concepts of the formal and informal organization they do not always use this knowledge when dealing with government bodies. It may be noted, however, that there is also a political dimension to interactions within the domain, and between it and other disciplines. The charge that psychologists tend to be "soft on power" often refers to the lack of awareness of this dimension in the management of their professional activities. Of course, individuals differ in this respect, so that there are always some entrepreneurs who succeed in developing new areas of the domain for themselves.

To summarize the arguments presented in this chapter, the domain of work psychology is shaped both by members of the profession and by outside influences. It is misleading to consider either of these groups without reference to the other. However, there is always a dominant faction which regulates the definition of the domain and its public image. Now that there are so many outside influences impinging on the domain, and the domain is much more complex and highly differentiated, future developments should not be left to chance. We suggest that there are far more opportunities to plan and structure the profession to meet future needs than have been recognized to date. We therefore advocate the establishment of some kind of forum to deal with these issues in a systematic way, although we are not suggesting that there is a blueprint which will apply to all countries. The contrasts between several European countries (cf. the illustrations from Poland, Italy, France and Germany in Section 2) make it clear that a universal prescription is impossible.

3 The Work Psychologist: Whose Servant?

A. Introduction

The individual psychologist at all stages of his or her career has strong feelings about the nature and content of his/her professional activities. Although new psychology graduates may feel less secure than their more experienced colleagues, they share a common definition of the field, i.e. what they can and should offer to society in a professional capacity. Linked with this there are clear ideas as to what they cannot and should not do; in other words they distinguish between what they consider is "good" practice and what quacks and charlatans do. These shared views do not mean there is complete consensus among members of the profession, but only a common core which probably has its origins in early training programmes.

As in all occupations, socialization is a never ending process whereby the individual psychologist is constantly exposed to a variety of influences which shape his or her outlook, values and conduct. This socialization involves two different reference groups, that is both occupational and organizational socialization is involved. As a result of training, membership of a professional organization, and through formal and informal links with other psychologists, the individual forms concepts of the profession as a whole. These interact with those deriving from his or her organizational role and the people with whom he or she associates in that context. For example, the psychologist who works in an academic setting is subject to pressures to engage in research and a value system which emphasizes extending the frontiers of knowledge. The psychologist employed in a large organization, on the other hand, is expected to contribute to short-term problem solving and to give advice on personnel and policy issues.

In the early years of work psychology this dual process of socialization was relatively unproblematic, as psychologists occupied a restricted number of roles and the environment in which they worked was comparatively stable. Over the last decade all this has changed. There have been developments, both within and outside the domain, the interaction of which make the current situation one of uncertainty, if not to say crisis, for psychologists in terms of their professional identity. The period has been one characterized by social, political, technological and economic upheaval throughout the world. Everywhere there has been a ferment of ideas and conflicting and competing ideologies, with people in all walks of life having to adapt to situations which they have never previously encountered. The past is no longer an adequate guide to the present, with traditional institutions and ideologies unable to match the demands resulting from new developments. In these circumstances, a search for new approaches and ways of coping with the resultant conflicts, together with a preoccupation with possible futures, is evident in many fields (e.g. Ackoff, 1974). Thus, in addition to those who maintain that the developed nations are moving from an industrial to a post-industrial society, there is growing awareness of the problems of managing and distributing resources to meet the demands and aspirations of the Third World. One much publicized example of something which may have profound consequences for the standard of living and lifestyle of the whole world is the energy crisis.

B.   The last twenty years

During the nineteen sixties one of the influential criticisms of American industrial psychologists and sociologists was published by Baritz (1965) under the title of *The Servants of Power*. This articulated the dependencies of these practitioners on management, particularly of big business, which undermined any claim on their part to operate with scientific detachment. In Europe, the same period saw the questioning of the underlying values of practitioners who were challenged to declare their interests. This was the time in which various radical criticisms of psychologists emerged and in which strongly humanistic values were subscribed to by student groups throughout the world. Student unrest came to a head in many countries in 1968 and 1969, in a public declaration of their rejection of traditional values. As a result, work psychologists, who had previously worked on problems of productivity and performance without feeling any embarrassment or guilt, were confronted by the need to justify their activities. Those who had never considered that they were "the lackeys of management" found that this was how they appeared to students and others, giving them restricted access to other groups in the sphere of work, e.g. trade unions.

Another much debated issue in that period was whether or not science is value free. Philosophers of science drew attention to the implicit values underlying scientific method, and in social science subjectivism became fashionable. Within psychology there was a revival of experiential approaches, with some psychologists turning away from the traditional scientific and positivistic methods in favour of more introspective and subjective analyses of behaviour. The latter group also rejected the role of the expert and stressed joint exploration and the individual's responsibility for his or her actions.

Over the same period the growth of the field and the diversification of jobs open to work psychologists meant that individuals had a far greater choice of ways of applying their knowledge. In particular, the development of interest in organizations, both as a topic of academic study and as a sphere of employment, widened the concepts of professional activities. It also involved psychologists in different client relationships, often of a complex kind.

The result of these developments was a critical and painful reappraisal of their position by work psychologists. It meant that the perspectives they had taken for granted had to be examined, and the legitimation of their activities had to be re-established. This entailed not only re-examination of methods and methodologies but also of customs and practices and modes of behaviour. In a number of professional associations there was strong pressure to formulate a code of ethics and much anxious discussion on matters such as the rights of employees to see confidential information about themselves. Inevitably this raised questions about on whose behalf psychologists were really working. Advocates of new ideologies, such as critical psychologists, took a prescriptive view and maintained that the only legitimate activities were those directed to improving the position of under-privileged workers. At the end of this period, which not only work psychologists found stressful and bewildering, role conflict had intensified and there was much ambiguity as to what constituted appropriate professional behaviour. For many work psychologists it was a question of trying to find their own way because there was no consensus of views amongst their colleagues. In essence then, from the beginning of the nineteen seventies, psychology has been in a period of transition. It is impossible to state with certainty which direction it will take during the nineteen eighties, but the following issues are clear.

1.   THE SCIENTIST'S VERSUS THE PRACTITIONER'S ROLE

Despite the growth in opportunities for practice, psychologists are trained to be scientists. This means that ideas concerning a systematic approach to well-defined problems, the control of variables, control of measurements, and operating with impartiality, are all part of the expectations engendered in students. At the same time, students are exposed to the values and ideologies subscribed to by their peers about the world of work and the economic and political structure of society. As indicated above, the tendency in recent years has been for these to take the form of radical criticism of the established order. Con-sequently, students are faced with contradiction from the beginning, i.e. the notion of scientific detachment, on the one hand, and the declared allegiance to specific values on the other. Furthermore, it is impossible for them to reconcile these positions by seeking to become practitioners rather than scientists, because practitioners are employed by and on behalf of management. However much we may deplore the fact, it is only at the executive and managerial level of an organization that decisions can be made to allocate resources to work psychologists and other specialists engaged in organizational problems. There is therefore a conflict. Younger members of the profession seek to put their knowledge to use on behalf of those whom they regard as the most needy members of society, a position which is ideological rather than scientific; but those with the power to commission their service are not the group whose interests they wish to further.

This raises the whole question of the legitimation of the work psychologist. Legitimation is not solely within the control of the profession, but is a process in which clients play an active part, both by commissioning the services of practitioners, and responding to the latter's claims to certain expertise. It involves mutual recognition by fellow members of the profession and by clients of the right to practise within a given area of the domain, which are substantiated by initial success in implementation and subsequent reinforcement of these activities. This reinforcement may take the form of repeat commissions by the client for the same services, and/or recommendation to other prospective clients. In this way, by a process of rewarding for certain activities, and failure to reward others leading to extinction, the client inadvertently shapes the practitioner's behaviour. At the same time the practitioner looks to other psychologists for approval in order to be reassured that what he is doing comes within the professional domain.

Following these initial developments, the next stage in the process is justified by reference to a system of shared values which have developed during the previous interaction. As a result, an ideology may develop, e.g. the humanization of work, to which it is assumed that all affected parties will subscribe. The past, and particularly the immediate past, is very influential in this respect, as noted by Helson in his Adaptation Level Theory (1964). This means, in effect, that a change of ideology is always imminent whenever an application does not conform to previous custom and practice. Attempts will then be made to reduce dissonance which may lead eventually to a new approach.

Another important function of the legitimation process is that it gives direction to current and future practice. It thus serves as a kind of shorthand to professional conduct, in the sense that clients and practitioners do not expect to, nor do they have to, spell out in detail all the dimensions of their relationship. However, when competing claims are made by rivals or illegitimate practitioners, they are immediately recognized as operating outside the boundaries of a particular legitimate terrain. These other groups themselves have an important role in defining the domain of the in-group. Were there not the contrast between the approved and non-approved claimants, the boundaries of the field would be extremely difficult to determine. In other words, it is as important to define the nature of "not A" as "A" in the process of legitimation. It would be impossible to define the virtuous if rogues did not exist.

2.   THE NATURE OF CLIENTS

The second issue relates to choice of client. As already noted, until the late sixties most psychologists believed implicitly that their contributions were both beneficial and useful to society and that, as long as clients were prepared to employ them, the value of their efforts was unquestioned. Occasional criticisms were apt to be attributed to ignorance on the part of the critic or the misconstruing of information, rather than to any inherent flaw or weakness in the psychologist's position. Although one or two individual psychologists were not prepared to work for certain clients (e.g. military, on conscientious grounds) in general there was no questioning within the profession about the nature of the client–practitioner relationship.

In the aftermath of the student protest and other upheavals, together with the emergence of active pressure groups of all kinds (e.g. feminists, racial equality groups, environmental lobbies, etc.), it is impossible for practitioners to avoid the question of values and their own allegiances. Nevertheless, the awareness of these issues does not mean that choice of clients is a simple matter for work psychologists. Even in academic institutions there are underlying assumptions and power relationships which affect the individual's activities. Whether we like it or not, whatever we do reinforces certain values, and fails to support others (e.g. it is widely held that employment is a more desirable state for a human being than unemployment). Therefore, it is not only at the point of decision as to whether or not to work for a particular client that personal values are involved, but they permeate all attitudes and behaviour. Very often colleague relationships and group memberships entail multiple loyalties which, themselves, represent some conflicting values. The person who holds a unitary ideological position which is sustained in all circumstances seems to be an abstraction.

The clients for whom psychologists work are rarely simple entities. They are usually complex systems, embracing a variety of groups with overlapping memberships, and different aspirations and values. The critics who maintain that psychological consultancy supports the establishment present an over-simplified view of the latter when they assume that its members have a unitary outlook. The tendency to reify organizations is clearly discernible in this context. In most countries the client groups who seek the help of psychologists fall under the following headings: government and local government agencies, industry, commercial organizations, social services, research institutions, educational institutions and, in a very few instances, trade union organizations. In certain circumstances, e.g. vocational guidance, they may also be individuals. This list illustrates the extension of the work psychologist's areas of practice as, in the early days, it was primarily industry which sought the help of work psychologists. Research data on the perceived responsibility and desirability of working for these different groups are rare, but individual members of the profession have their own pecking order. So too do students and fellow social scientists. In an unpublished study done in the early seventies, de Wolff found that work psychology students showed a clear order of preference for employment in, first, universities; second, government agencies; third, industrial organizations. For established teachers and practitioners the importance attached to different clients is likely to vary with circumstances, e.g. during an economic recession there is a tendency to look for support from and to work for government bodies on the grounds that these are more likely to have funds available than any other institution.

The situations which give rise to contracts between clients and practitioners, whether of a research or consultancy nature, are many and diverse. Although it is frequently assumed that the sponsoring body makes a formal approach to the practitioner, who may then decide whether or not to accept this assignment, in practice formal approaches usually follow much informal contact and discussion. There is a large element of chance in the way in which certain queries and problems are directed to certain informal networks. Furthermore, although some practitioners are more active than others in seeking to sell their services, it would be difficult to identify any well-worn path which leads to the initiation of certain programmes.

3. THE NATURE OF PROBLEMS

In general work psychologists are attracted by problems to which they feel their theoretical knowledge and practical skills are relevant. Clients are also anxious to find solutions to problems, but the latter are often presented in forms which are not amenable to psychological investigation without some re-definition, e.g. government bodies may commission research as a way of delaying making a particular policy decision. It is seldom that any commissioned research project is undertaken without negotiation between sponsors and practitioners with a view to reaching an agreed definition of the problem and the terms of reference. However, a fundamental discrepancy often remains, in that psychologists tend to look at the situation in rational terms, whereas the clients' concerns tend to be primarily political. Thus, psychologists tend to see their role as that of applying scientific knowledge and techniques to well-defined problems, whereas clients are usually more concerned with expediency and strengthening their particular position. Regardless of whether the client organization is in the public or private sector, it is subject to multiple pressures through being in competition with others for resources and having to satisfy powerful and competing interests. Consequently, it is not surprising that problems are generally viewed against this background and are apt to be formulated in political terms.

The kind of problems which students and those of a humanistic persuasion want to solve are of a different order. These usually relate to the structuring of society as a whole and the position of disadvantaged groups. Such problems can only be formulated in macro-terms, i.e. they are not available to investigation or solution by psychological methods. Herein lies one contradiction for those who believe that their subject can benefit others: they find that the extent to which, as professionals, they can bring about change is limited to the micro-level. To fulfil their ambitions for a better world, these idealists have to operate as "political animals" rather than as scientists or practitioners. Humanistic psychologists are usually well aware of the nature of their bias and of the impossibility of approaching large-scale societal problems with scientific detachment. However, in consultancy, although practitioners may think that their professional code of conduct protects them from compromise with positions to which they do not subscribe themselves, in practice they cannot always avoid such compromise. As indicated above, there is a political dimension to negotiations with and working on behalf of clients which work psychologists should not ignore. In other words, they have to accept that they are engaging in collaborative problem-solving with those whose values may be very different from their own and to acknowledge the consequences.

4. QUESTIONS OF VALUE

Philosophers of science have pointed out that, even within the context of a rigorous controlled scientific experiment, subjectivity is entailed in the interpretation of data. Furthermore the choice of research topics often reflects the particular interests and values of the investigator. It is, therefore, not simply that questions of value affect only those psychologists engaged as practitioners, but they permeate scientific activities as well. It is sometimes suggested that practitioners should be judged according to how far their behaviour is governed solely by the pursuit of truth and scientific endeavour. This is to grossly oversimplify the psychologist's position. Not only is scientific detachment more an ideal than a practical position, but other values and responsibilities are also involved. Administrative procedures for the allocation of resources, responsibilities for subordinates and the development of their careers, together with obligations to maintain and defend the boundaries of the domain, are some of the influences compelling the psychologist to act politically as well as scientifically, e.g. the professor who fails to secure research funds for his department will be criticized by both colleagues and students, who may not realize how much negotiating and cultivating of influential sponsors may have to go into this activity.

All organizations may be considered in terms of the competing values of their members. Also, as Burns (1968) has pointed out, organizations represent a plurality of social systems. Thus, at a minimum, there is a task system, a career system, and a political system associated with competition for resources and battles for power. All members of an organization are part of all these three systems and probably others as well. Consequently, while individuals are performing their jobs they are also seeking to advance their own careers and forming coalitions with other groups to further the influence of their own departments.

Psychologists have not been immune from this activity, although it is rare to find them acknowledging the fact, because they tend to believe that the theoretical formulations underpinning their activities legitimize them in scientific terms. For example, a number of well-known theories of leadership style have been advocated on the ground of research findings, rather than in terms of their latent ideology. There are always at least two reference groups to which the work psychologist looks for approval, i.e. his professional peers and his clients, neither of which is homogeneous. One consequence of this situation is that psychologists are not the servants of any one master. If they wish to remain within the profession they must demonstrate to their peers that they are abreast of the latest developments in the field, and prepared to engage in scientific debate with their fellows. Concerning their clients they have to interpret their data and recommendations in accordance with the overall objectives of the organization, including being willing to commit themselves to the merit of particular courses of action. To their students they have to be credible, well-informed and sympathetic to the ideals of the younger generation, for if they do not encourage others to follow in their footsteps the profession runs the risk of withering away.

These conflicting allegiances, however, have their positive aspects. Too great a commitment to any one faction isolates those concerned from intellectual challenge and creative conflict. In psychology, as in other subjects, examples can be found of the corrupting influences of popularity and commercial success which have made some initially fruitful ideas sterile. Although it is difficult to look to different "masters", their multiplicity can prevent rigidity and preoccupation with irrelevant issues.

5. PERSONAL IDENTITY

These considerations lead us to the view that role ambiguity and role conflict are inherent in the profession of work psychology. In accordance with the findings of Kahn *et al.* (1964) one can discern the ways in which some psychologists have been affected by these problems of role, e.g. by feeling that their activities are futile and by adopting avoidance strategies. Similarly, there is evidence that role conflicts can weaken the bonds of trust between the professional and his superiors at some cost to both the individual and the organization.

However, there may also be positive responses. The need to resolve role conflict and/or role ambiquity can lead to creative activities and the pushing forward of the frontiers of knowledge. Innovation and originality may be stimulated by differences of opinion between individuals, groups or organizations. Fundamentally, it seems to be a question of the work psychologist discovering and having confidence in his or her own identity. Although membership of the profession, code of professional conduct, close association with professional colleagues, and so on, provides support and guidelines, ultimately one has to make a personal choice. The only guarantee of quality in the final analysis is the individual's personal integrity.

References

ACKOFF, R. L. (1974). *Redesigning the Future — A Systems Approach to Societal Problems.* Wiley, New York.

BARITZ, L. (1960). *The Servants of Power.* Wesleyan University Press, Middletown, Connecticut.

BARRY, B., SHACKLETON, V. and LANSLEY, P. (1978). Management and industrial relations research in British academic centres. *Management International Review* 18, 83-96 and 18, 87-100.

BAUMGARTEN-TRAMER, F. (1971). Chronologie des entwicklung der arbeitswissenschaft und der angewandten psychologie. *Arbeitswissenschaft,* 8/9, 165-182.

BENNIS, W. G., BENNE, K. D. and CHIN, R. (eds) (1964). *The Planning of Change,* Readings in the Applied Behavioural Sciences. Holt, Rinehart and Winston, New York.

BURNS, T. (1966). On the plurality of social systems. In *Operational Research and the Social Sciences* (Lawrence, J. R., ed.). Tavistock Publications, London.

CAMPBELL, J. P., CAMPBELL, R. J., SCHEIN, V. E. AND THAYER, P. W. (1976). Report of the Long-Range Planning Committee, Division 14, A.P.A. (mimeograph).

DE MONTMOLLIN, M. (1978). Quelques aspects de la psychologie industrielle aux USA en 1977. *Bulletin de Psychologie,* XXXI, 12-15.

DE WOLFF, C. J. (1977). *Uit de ivoren toren.* Van Loghum Slaterus, Deventer.

DE WOLFF, C. J. AND SHIMMIN, S. (1976). The psychology of work in Europe: A review of a profession. *Personnel Psychology,* 29, 175-195.

DAVIDSON, M. A. (1977). The scientific/applied debate in psychology: A contribution. *Bulletin of the British Psychological Society,* 30, 273-278.

DRENTH, P. J. D. (1978). Arbeids-en organisatie psychologie. In *Psychologie Vandaag* (Duijker, H. C. J., ed.). Van Loghum Slaterus, Deventer.

52   1. THE DOMAIN OF WORK PSYCHOLOGY

DUNNETTE, M. D. (ed.) (1976). *Handbook of Industrial and Organisational Psychology*. Rand McNally, Chicago.
DUIJKER, H. C. J. (1977). De psychologie en haar toekomst. *De Psycholoog*, **XII**, 353-358.
ELDEN, J. M. (1978). Participatory research leads to employee-managed change. In *Working on the Quality of Working Life — Reports and Notes on Twenty-nine Current Innovative Improvement Efforts in Eight European Countries* (Alioth, A., Blake, J., Bulteriss, M., Elden, M., Ortsman, O. and van der Vlist, R., eds). Martinus Nijhoff, Leiden.
EMERY, F. E. AND THORSRUD, E. (1969). *Form and Content in Industrial Democracy*. Tavistock Publications, London.
EMERY, F. E. AND TRIST, E. L. (1965). The causal texture of organizational environments. *Human Relations*, **18**, 21-32.
HELLER, F. A. (1976). Towards a practical psychology of work. *Journal of Occupational Psychology*, **49**, 45-54.
HELSON, H. (1964). *Adaption-level Theory: An Experimental and Systematic Approach to Behaviour*. Harper and Row, New York.
HOCH, E. A. (1962). Psychology today: Conceptions and misconceptions. In *The Profession of Psychology* (Webb, W. B., ed.). Holt, Rinehart and Winston, New York.
JAQUES, E. (1951). *The Changing Culture of a Factory*. Tavistock Publications, London.
KAHN, R. L., WOLFF, D. M., QUINN, R. P. AND SNOEK, J. D. (1964). *Organizational Stress: Studies in Role Conflict and Ambiguity*. Wiley, New York.
KRIJNEN, G. (1975, 1976). *Ontwikkeling Funktievervulling van Psychologen*, I and II. I.T.S., Nijmegen.
LEPLAT, J. (1971). La psychologie du travail. In *Traite de Psychologie Appliquée* (Reuchlin, M., ed.). Presses Universitaires de France, Paris.
MCKINNEY, F. (1976). Fifty years of psychology, *American Psychologist*, **31**, 834-842.
MCCOLLUM, I. M. (1960). Psychologists in industry in the United Kingdom and Western Germany, *American Psychologist*, **15**, 58-64.
MOK, A. L. (1973). *Beroepen in Actie*. Boom, Meppel.
NEDERLANDS INSTITUUT VAN PSYCHOLOGEN (1976). *Beroepsethiek voor Psychologen*, Leden van het N.I.P., Amsterdam.
PETZ, B. Ausbilding und Tätigkeit Jugoslawischer Betriebspsychologoen. Conference paper. Mimeograph.
RIESMAN, D. (1950). *The Lonely Crowd*. Yale University Press, New Haven.
SEMINARA, J. L. (1976). Psychology in Bulgaria, *Bulletin of the British Psychological Society*, **29**, 143-149.
SOCIAL SCIENCE RESEARCH COUNCIL (1975). *Research in Organizational Behaviour: A British Survey* by D. S. Pugh, R. Mansfield and M. Warner. Heinemann Educational Books, London.
SPALTRO, E. (1974). *Storia e Metodo della Psicologia del Lavaro*. Etas Libri, Milano.

THOMPSON, J. D. (1967). *Organizations in Action.* McGraw Hill, New York.
THORSRUD, E. (1972). Job design in the wider context. In *Design of Jobs* (Davis, L. E. and Taylor, J. C., eds). Penguin Books, Harmondsworth.
VARELA, J. A. (1975). Can social psychology be applied? In *Applying Social Psychology — Implications for Research, Practice and Training* (Deutsch, M. and Hornstein, H. A., eds). Lawrence Erlbaum Associates, Hillsdale, N.J.
VAN VUCHT TIJSSEN, VAN DER BROECKE, A. A. J., VAN DIJKHUIZEN, M., REICHE, H. M. I. K. L., DE WOLFF, C. J. (1978). *Middenkader en Stress.* C.O.P., 's-Gravenhage.

Section 2
The Domain of Work Psychology: Some Illustrations

edited by

SYLVIA SHIMMIN and CHARLES J. DE WOLFF

Introduction

SYLVIA SHIMMIN and CHARLES J. DE WOLFF

This section contains chapters by authors who do not usually publish in the English Language. Nearly all have had to be translated and edited, a situation which has not been without its difficulties. The editors are very conscious that much of the "flavour" of the original is lost in translation and, as a result, similarities between countries may appear greater than is actually the case. Chapters 4 to 6 describe the position of work psychology in West Germany, Italy and Poland. Heinz-Ludwig Horney, who is a professor at the Advanced Mining School at Bochum, is the first contributor. Chapter 5 is written by Enzo Spaltro of the University of Bologna, who is currently the President of the Italian Psychological Association. Marian Dobrzyński of the University of Warsaw is the author of Chapter 6.

Although these three countries differ widely in their culture, history and educational philosophy, nevertheless it is apparent that some of the issues discussed in Section 1 occur in a similar form in all these countries. These contributions illustrate both the variety and the similarity to be found in work psychology throughout Europe.

Chapters 7 and 8 deal with more specific parts of the domain, ergonomics and personnel selection, each within the context of a particular country. Jean-Claude Sperandio, professor at the University of Paris VIII describes psychological ergonomics in France, and Charles de Wolff discusses issues relating to personnel selection in the Netherlands.

These are followed by a Swedish contribution. In this, Professor

Göran Ekvall describes a study which attempts to forecast what working life in Sweden may be like in the nineteen-nineties. A feature of interest in the latter is the lack of agreement between judges about future developments with respect to opportunities for self-realization at work.

The title of our book, *Conflicts and Contradictions*, is therefore borne out in these different illustrations. Each author indicates the potential of work psychology, on the one hand, but, on the other, makes clear that it is a highly complex field, in which there are no simple solutions.

4 Work Psychology in West Germany

HEINZ-LUDWIG HORNEY

A. A brief backward glance (historical survey)

The first blossoming of German research in work psychology occurred between the two World Wars, especially in the twenties and thirties.

In many universities and technical universities (Academies), after the so-called "Psychotechnics" had been outgrown and discarded, many fruitful research attempts were undertaken, the results of which have been felt throughout the world and up to the present time. In particular, investigations of human performance, fatigue, rest-pauses, causes of accidents, the development of working methods (machinery), monotony of work on the conveyor belt, vocational education, youth, women and the middle-aged at work, as well as of team work, laid the foundation for present-day industrial research. This research was carried out in close operation with interested engineers and members of the medical profession, largely because many of the researchers were members of the teaching staff of technical university departments. In addition to those researchers mentioned by McCollom (1960), the following were actively involved: N. Ach, F. Baumgarten, H. Dueker, F. Giese, O. Graf, B. Herwig, W. Hische, E. Kraepelin, K. Lewin, O. Lipmann, K. Marbe, W. Moede, M. Moers, A. Ruessel, H. Rupp. Stimulating ideas also came from Great Britain, France, Switzerland and the USA.

Subsequent political events and the Second World War led to the emigration of a number of scientists causing a noticeable decline in both research and practical applications. A ray of light came with the introduction, in 1942, of an examination course in psychology leading to a professional Diploma which unified the studies and which, with some modifications, is still valid today.

Reconstruction after the Second World War in the now divided Germany led, in some places, to a vigorous rebirth of activity, above all in the field of work psychology. This was due to a lively demand from many spheres of the economy. An important stimulus was provided by the Forschungsinstitut für Arbeitspsychologie und Personalwesen — FORFA (Research Institute for Work Psychology and Personnel Management), founded by B. Herwig in Braunschweig and Dusseldorf (1948) which carried out basic research, aptitude testing and also trained managerial personnel. Until its dissolution in 1963 it employed in succession some 50 psychologists and, above all, provided young new graduates with an opportunity to get some first-hand practical experience. Thanks to the pioneering work of this institute, work psychology in West Germany still has a good reputation.

Other spheres of activity opened up at the employment offices (run by the Government) and at the institutes of technical supervisory unions responsible for the fitness of transport personnel. At the same time, large and medium-sized enterprises began to employ psychologists whose job consisted of selection and training. They also acted as personnel managers.

This post-war phase was greatly influenced by research results, stemming mainly from the USA, which helped to shape the hitherto traditional German field of application concerned with aptitude testing, training, and working conditions. As early as the twenties the ideas of Taylor and Gilbreth were critically examined. Now the field was enlarged by modern test theories and statistics, and the results of social psychology were applied to problems of management behaviour, motivation and organizational development. The psychology of personality, emphasizing the totality of man, was already well-established in Germany so that continuity of development in this sphere has been maintained.

B.   Present-day figures (statistics)

The lively development of psychology can be seen from the following figures. In 1979, 17 000 students were studying psychology as their major degree subject at 33 universities and technical universities in West Germany; 670 of these were postgraduate candidates for a doctorate ($= 3\cdot9\%$). The *Diplom-Psychologe* needs 5-6 years' study, and another 2-3 years is necessary for the doctorate. Because of the demand for places these were allocated on the basis of a *numerus fixus*. (In comparison, Austria has 3200 students and 550 postgraduates, and Switzerland 1700 students and 178 postgraduates.)

In the Professional Association of German Psychologists, more than 5000 colleagues are organized at present; of these some 600 belong to the division of Industrial Psychology. As membership is voluntary one could add to this number another 600 practising industrial psychologists who are not members of the association.

The division of Industrial Psychology for the past 20 years has held annual three-day conferences which provide for further education of its members and the dissemination of information to the public at large. Specific work teams in this section concern themselves with scrutiny of legislative proposals, with safety at work, with psychology of organizations, psychology of the disabled etc. in order to safeguard the interests of members and — in cooperation with other organizations — to solve problems of mutual interest. Considering the availability of programmes in psychology it becomes obvious that very few offer work psychology as such, because 80-90% of the students prefer clinical psychology in spite of a marked decrease in job opportunities. The lack of interest in work psychology may be attributed to the following facts: clinical psychology being both more fashionable and attractive, aversion to industrial work, lack of information about real tasks and employment opportunities and last, but not least, to the limited opportunity to study the subject. Only a few universities provide courses in work psychology, i.e. Hamburg, Frankfurt, Munich, Freiburg, Berlin.

C. Focal points of research

There are numerous research projects being undertaken at the above mentioned universities and also at some other institutes. However, the total volume of research is unsatisfactory. Without claiming completeness or suggesting an order of importance, work is going on in the following areas: problems of job analysis; engineering psychology (human engineering, human factors); job satisfaction; aptitudes, professional training; motivation; decision-making procedures; shiftwork, nightwork; training in safety; measures of accident prevention; training methods for managerial staff; changes in managerial behaviour; new technologies and organizational development; reintegration of the unemployed into the work process. Allied to these are specific investigations within the framework of governmental programmes into the "quality of working life", mostly in cooperation with other specialized disciplines. Here work psychology is still under-represented, with industrial sociologists often doing research with a psychological slant.

Reasons for the poor participation of industrial psychologists in certain research programmes are hard to identify. One reason may be lack of sponsorship from official organizations, as well as from industry. Another may be the spread of psychological teaching to students of other disciplines, for example an increase in the number of higher educational establishments, such as *Gesamthochschulen*, training colleges, vocational colleges, which offer psychology as a subsidiary subject. There is also a tendency by economists, sociologists, engineers, medical officers, and even theologians, to take over psychological activities. Although this frequently leads to a fruitful cross-fertilization of ideas it also leads to the blurring of territorial boundaries: mistakes are then often blamed on psychologists. At the same time, the professional field of work psychology is becoming broader, with psychologists engaged in educational tasks and personnel management, or as members of boards of directors or consulting firms. Some of the favourite spheres of activity by non-psychologists are training of managerial staff, investigations into job satisfaction, job evaluation, problems of job security etc. This is reflected also in publications whereby particular findings of industrial psychologists from the USA are taken over and applied without discrimination. Their one-sidedness is often not appreciated, neither are the possible consequences of their mis-application.

In recent years universities have been endeavouring to provide further specialized training for practising industrial psychologists in order to publicize the newest findings and to enable industries to make use of them. This programme is still being developed.

D. Tasks of industrial psychologists in their field

According to Friederichs (1978), workers and managers are looking to industrial psychologists for help in the following five areas:

1. selection and placement of employees, vocational guidance, reduction of absenteeism, and of disruptions to production, bearing in mind the costs involved;
2. optimization of management skills such as communication, cooperation, avoidance of group conflicts, meaningful performance motivation;
3. maintaining the health of workers through guidance and attention to working conditions and safety;
4. influencing the social climate through clearly defined modes of conduct and management principles, decision-making processes, and a fair structure of social service benefits;
5. maintenance of a stable level of employment through consultation, retraining and job mobility.

Of the industrial psychologists 80% are employed in firms of over 2000 employees. In the smaller firms only 12% employ psychologists. In accordance with the Work Safety Act a ratio of one doctor per 3500 workers is laid down; if one applies a similar standard for psychologists then at present there is a shortfall of some 6000 psychologists.

The majority of industrial psychologists work in the chemical industries, in iron and steel companies and in the electrical industries, 10% in mining and vehicle-producing industries, and the rest are employed in textile firms, banks and insurance and in food production and consumer goods. Of the 100 most productive German enterprises, some 50 are employing one or more psychologists.

There is a conspicuous gap between work psychologists in industry and the universities. Very few practising industrial psychologists undertake lecturing assignments at universities although they have a keen interest in new scientific findings.

The largest number of psychologists (some 250) is to be found in the employment offices, in the Armed Forces (180) and in the transport assessment centres (some 160). Most of these would regard themselves as belonging to the field of industrial psychology.

The job satisfaction of work psychologists is generally good in comparison with other groups of practitioners. They enjoy favourable working conditions which they have created largely through their own efforts and initiative. It also shows that their efforts have brought them esteem and recognition. One may therefore attribute their job satisfaction to the following factors: independence; job security; variety and diversity of tasks; professional prestige; organizational "climate"; income; social prestige.

What positions are occupied by work psychologists in organizations? Some 71% are engaged in psychological work, 15% in vocational education, 10% work as personnel managers and 4% are in senior executive positions. In this respect, there is some similarity to the United States, where trained psychologists engage in a variety of tasks and activities. However, increasing legislation means that the psychologist in industry has to deal with a series of statutory regulations, e.g. the Industrial Administration Act, which envisages far-reaching rights of participation by the Workers' Council, especially with regard to personnel affairs; the Professional Training Act, with its rules on internal training, retraining and further development; the Work Safety Act, with regulations regarding industrial physicians and specially trained safety personnel (not, however, psychologists!). The Act concerned with the creation of humane working conditions, including consideration of the psychological aspects of employment, has greatly influenced the activity of the German Institute for Standardization (DIN). This has introduced standards for Human Engineering (Ergonomics) for use by the working committees on which psychologists are numerically well represented and active participants.

To give some idea of the relative participation rates in different activities, if we take 100 for full-time involvement then the order of magnitude is as follows: aptitude testing and system evaluation (35%); vocational training, education (20%); ergonomics, work safety, organizational development (20%); counselling of workers (10%); research into staffing (10%); others (5%). Within this context there is a growing emphasis on a number of specific projects, for example: problem-solving techniques, in relation to their development, introduction, training, control and supervision; appraisal systems, including staff-development programmes; job design, which includes interdisciplinary approaches to job structuring, group formation and man–machine systems, e.g. jobs involving computer displays, supervisory activities, and jobs with high accident risks; continuing education and training, including the application of modern teaching methods in effecting communication and organizational structures.

Overall, while it may appear that work psychology in practice seems to be highly effective there are still few firms employing psychologists or which are prepared to engage them. Where psychologists are already at work, their number is growing, so that focal groups have been formed (in chemical plants, the electrical industry, iron and steel companies) with their own systems and close cooperation. Unfortunately, their many activities and results remain unpublished because of lack of time and opportunity. As a result non-psychologists rely on popular and often misunderstood, misleading, one-sided or exaggerated publications, knowing little or nothing of the authentic work and uses of work psychology.

E. Current trends

In recent years two parallel trends seem to be emerging: on the one hand, the tendency "to give psychology away" seems to prevail, with its aim to acquaint others with specifically psychological knowledge whenever they so desire and, on the other hand, the aim is to train psychologists predominantly for research. Teachers at universities and colleges follow both trends according to their individual preferences and opportunities.

Thus, there are many questions posed to which answers have still to be found. In particular, these relate to the competence of psychology and of psychologists. There is no statutory protection governing the practice of psychology so that both those holding the *Diplom-Psychologe* and those without it are allowed to practise without any restriction — for the benefit or detriment of others. A Code of Professional Ethics exists, but this is binding only for members of the Professional Association of German Psychologists. Recently "basic principles for aptitude testing" were formulated by the Division of Industrial Psychology. These are intended to prevent abuses of "testing" in industry, to guide colleagues and to inform clients.

One should stress again the relatively small number of students who desire to take up industrial psychology, which may be due to the limited opportunities (at universities) or it may be due to lack of demand. What can be regarded as cause and what as effect is difficult to establish. Frequently one finds that graduates are well endowed theoretically but are lacking in vision as to what can be achieved in the practical field. The right time when, and by whom, initiation into practical work should take place has to be carefully assessed to ensure that the transfer from academic study to the field of practice is not too difficult and to avoid disappointments, failures and insecurity. To date, no one has given a thought as to what is to become of the 3000 graduates expected each year, nor the consequences of training them regardless of job opportunities.

The role of work psychologists in industrial relations is largely unproblematic because details concerning co-determination in personnel affairs are regulated by law. As far as can be seen, there is more cooperation than confrontation. Some psychologists are employed by unions, or even by workers' councils, others by employers' organizations. Although this leads to different points of view, psychologists working within companies are generally not faced with basic problems of employer–employee relations. They operate largely on the basis of their professional knowledge and experience.

Industrial psychology now faces many challenges. Technological developments are affecting both the nature and structure of employment. Employees are making higher claims and — as always in times of crisis — new values are being sought, which will inevitably shape the future. Thus work psychology mirrors the conflicts and contradictions of its time. Three particular areas are:

1. designing work-conditions with a view to demand, motivation, aptitude, training, and work-structuring;

2. organizational design, especially with regard to enterprise structure, motivation, cooperation and decision making;

3. self-realization at work, including a critical analysis of its aims, methods and limitations.

Finally, one becomes aware, in retrospect, that many current problems originated in the past, but there is now greater knowledge available to deal with them. It is essential to come to grips with problems, such as the effects of labour law, of the enterprise economy, of electronic computer data processing, industrial training and safety at work. These have to be seen in the context of demographic factors — the aged, disabled, guest workers (in the second generation) — and of unemployment and the changing demands of technology. In other words, work psychology in the German Federal Republic today has to deal with complexity and tension.

References

FRIEDERICHS, P. (1978). Arbeits- und Betriebspsychologie in Wirtschaft und Verwaltung der Bundesrepublik Deutschland (Industrial psychology in the German Federal Republic). In *Arbeits- und Betriebspsychologie in der Bundesrepublik Deutschland — Stand und Perspektiven*, B.D.P., Duisberg, 15-36.

HORNEY, H. L. (1978). Berufsstandische und rechtliche Situation der Arbeits- und Betriebspsychologie in der Bundesrepublik Deutschland (Professional status and legal problems of industrial psychology in the German Federal Republic). In *Arbeits- und Betriebspsychologie in der Bundesrepublik Deutschland — Stand und Perspektiven*, B.D.P., Duisberg, 47-63.

MCCOLLOM, I. N. (1960). Industrial psychology in Great Britain and West Germany. *The American Psychologist*, 15, 58-64.

5 Industrial and Organizational Psychology in Italy: The Situation in 1978

ENZO SPALTRO

A. Introduction

Any summary of this kind is biased by the particular point of view of the writer and his personal convictions and feelings. So, in describing the situation of Italian industrial psychology in 1978, I am influenced by having been in the midst of efforts, fights and daily practical achievements in this field for a long time. In this short account, attention is given to influences shaping the psychology of work (*Psicologia del Lavoro*) in Italy in the last two decades to accord with the emphasis of other chapters in this book.

B. Historical background

In the early 1960s, no one in Italy was teaching work psychology in the universities. The first chair in industrial psychology was established in the Economics Faculty, Catholic University of Milano (E. Spaltro) in 1965, followed by another chair in the Sociology Faculty, Trento University, in 1967.

The strikes and riots in industry and the universities in the "hot autumn" of 1969 led to the closure of universities for many months and both the Italian Society of Psychology and the Association of Italian Industrial Psychology were dissolved. Although the former was re-established in 1973, the latter has not been revived.

In 1971 two courses in psychology were started in Padua and in Rome. Neither included the psychology of work, but the presence of these two existing faculties of psychology was destined to have a strong influence on the development of industrial psychology in Italy.

Other events of importance about this time include the law on the rights of workers "Bill no. 300", entitling them to 150 hours professional training per year, which highlighted the contribution which psychologists could make to training. It also prohibited opinion surveys among workers so that the professional activities of work psychologists did not develop, as elsewhere, through personnel selection and motivation research, but were directed towards ergonomics and organizational design and development.

After 1970, the political situation in Italy was pushing psychologists, little by little, to take a more responsible role. More chairs and teaching programmes had been established in the meanwhile and the Italian Society of Psychology developed a definition of the role of work psychologist (ergonomic tasks in design, group techniques, sociotechnical systems expert, etc.) at its 1977 Congress. However, the political situation, linked with the deteriorating economic situation, has meant that, since 1975, the hopes of psychology making more impact on industry and on working problems have been considerably reduced.

C.   Training of work psychologists

In 1976–7 there were some 18 000 students of psychology at the Universities of Rome and Padua, which are the only two giving a first degree in the subject. Some universities offer a 3-year postgraduate course for graduates in medicine and philosophy but, up to now, there has been no specific training in industrial and organizational psychology. Specialist schools, established with a professional aim in industrial psychology, have been forced to adopt a more generalist approach or, although officially recognized, they are not functioning for a number of reasons. In economics and engineering faculties an increasing curiosity can be discerned about psychological approaches to systems design. A stronger interest in work psychology exists in management schools and in the training departments run by unions for their representatives, but the latter tend to reject psychological methods as "strange", ineffective and part of management.

Given these circumstances, the problems of providing psychology students with sufficiently high standards of training are enormous and, in the professional industrial and organizational field, the immediate future does not appear optimistic.

D. Activities of work psychologists

If we want to understand what Italian psychologists are doing in the industrial and organizational area, it is necessary to recognize three groups of specialists: those who identify themselves as work psychologists; general psychologists who work in industry but who stress the scientific, rather than the applied, nature of their work; and those who occupy various functional roles, e.g. as personnel officers or union representatives. The last group comprises those who want to act like psychologists but, at the same time, to deny any association with the subject or the profession in the interests of power seeking, because industrial psychology in Italy carries low status.

Surveys undertaken by the Italian Society of Psychology have shown great variety in the activities and training of work psychologists, including some employed without training in this area at all. The "self-defining" group provided data suggesting that work psychology in Italy is largely a masculine job and a middle-aged profession. Only a few psychologists are employed full-time, partly because this carries overtones of being a "servant of power", and most work alone, although there are several consultancies and private institutions employing small groups of psychologists.

Research in industrial psychology is very rare and is mainly sponsored by special research foundations. Italian work psychology has rejected the classical tradition of industrial psychology in other countries, based on testing, job description, professional profiles and so on. In trying to become a profession, it is now accumulating a lot of technical know-how in the fields of organizational development, organizational diagnosis and climates, the management of conflict, the use of groups for training and for changing goals, and is seeking to provide a helping role for people confronted by problems of change. If we think of the equation *Efficiency = Production/Human Effort*, Italian work psychology is directed towards the increasing of efficiency through the decreasing of human effort, i.e. how to work less to produce more.

E. New trends

Due to the critical and divided economic and political circumstances, with the former showing some improvement while the latter continues to deteriorate, the domain of work psychology in Italy is now very narrow. In the next few years we need to strengthen membership of the professional association, define clearly and establish legal recognition of the role of the psychologist, develop a more efficient system of training and a more integrated labour market.

The central topic for Italian work psychology is the problem of the "Italian way" to organization, i.e. reaching new forms of co-living and working together which take into account not only structures and norms but feelings and behaviour, and which are culturally relevant. We cannot use models or methods developed elsewhere because the logic is different, e.g. the traditional (largely American) industrial psychology approach leaves no room for subjectivity and the "subjective" dimensions of work as we see them. It is the area of conflict, which characterizes all organizations, which is increasingly the sphere of our psychological practice. The future hopes for Italian psychologists in this field lie in training (connected with bargaining behaviour, organizational behaviour, decision making, risk taking, power equalization strategies and so on); organizational changes (through the management of change and conflict); and through efficiency achieved with decreasing human costs. In Italy, we speak often of the quality of life, not the quality of "working" life. This approach aims to connect work and non-work as a whole experience and may be seen as the core of both Italian work psychology and of Italian psychological work.

6 Work Psychology in Poland

MARIAN DOBRZYŃSKI

A. Historical background

In Poland, as elsewhere, the development of industrial psychology reflects the social situation and problems which confront society as a whole. The year 1918 saw the Renaissance of Poland as an independent state after 123 years of slavery. This meant that the country was confronted with the problem of integration of its population, divided by the cultural, legal and economic legacies of three invaders, representing different administrative systems and cultural traditions. One consequence was that applicants for work differed according to their geographic origins and, as such, were "unknown quantities" to the managers responsible for recruitment and selection. Although the over-population of the country enabled managers to select the "right" workers by a process of trial and error, in Poland, as in Western Europe and the USA, pre-conditions emerged for the development of psychological assessment procedures in selection.

The inter-war period saw psychotechnics flourishing in Poland, following pioneering work in the early 1920s. In 1917 Józefa Joteyko published a critical study of Taylorian "Scientific Management". She argued for consideration of the interest of workers as well as of managers, stating that the industrial psychologist's task is not only the raising of efficiency but also, and first of all, to satisfy the worker by providing him with a creative job, suited to his abilities. The same author also published research reports on stress caused by mental work, on fatigue, on the methodology of testing and other topics. A study in the Polish wood industry by Biegeleisen-Zelazowski in 1920, who designed apparatus for testing the abilities of workers and allocating them to jobs on the basis of their individual abilities, was a progressive step towards a vocational guidance approach which compared favourably with the one-sided selection procedures prevalent at that time.

The first Institute of Psychotechnics was established in Cracow in 1920. Then, in 1926, the Polish Psychotechnical Society was created which, as one of the first in Europe, from 1927 up to the Second World War issued regularly the quarterly "Psychotechnika" and organized annual congresses of Polish psychotechnicians. A lasting expression of the Society's achievements was the setting up of a number of psychotechnic centres in railways, industry and vocational schools. At this time, the main fields of activity for psychologists were testing, vocational guidance and the improvement of psychophysical conditions of work. Their tests and instruments were largely adopted from the United States and France and worked out for use in Poland.

After the Second World War, from 1949 until the late 1950s, psychology in Poland was restricted to the limits of Pavlovian neurophysiology and the activity of psychologists in industry was confined to the prevention of accidents. The contemporary development of work psychology dates from the end of this period, when psychological laboratories were set up once again in industry.

Thus, in the late 1950s, the changing political situation led to a sudden enlivenment of Polish industrial psychology. Publications on the subject appeared in Polish, based on foreign literature, but later containing reports on Polish research. A tendency to accept Western ideas uncritically was apparent, stimulated by social scientists and managers themselves travelling to the West. Interest in applications, such as human relations and testing as a powerful tool of employee selection, was very great and managers often had unrealistic expectations as to what psychologists could offer. During the first half of the 1960s, therefore, numerous laboratories were established at big industrial plants, e.g. in foundries, mines and the engineering industry, but these declined in the second half of the decade as managers became disappointed with the psychologists' inability to provide instant solutions to the problems presented to them.

A similar pattern of tremendous opportunity for work psychology, followed by inability to measure up to expectations, marks the 1970s. The change of accent in social and economic policy after 1970, characterized by concern about the quality of life and the launching of a number of courageous development programmes, provided many openings and opportunities for social scientists, including psychologists. Practically unlimited resources were made available for research and new laboratories in business organizations and research institutes founded.

Unfortunately, industrial psychologists were not able to react creatively to this surprising challenge, so their share in the utilization of these resources was rather modest. They were unable to meet the challenge because they were neither sufficiently organized nor could they offer qualified services. All they could provide were some attractive ideas about improving the quality of working life, management development, personnel management and so on. Meanwhile, the gap left by psychologists was invaded by various newcomers identified as economists, sociologists, organization theorists, or people who were not identified professionally at all. These individuals undertook research programmes, management training, consultancies and published books on organizational behaviour even more frequently than psychologists themselves.

By the mid 1970s it became evident that the resources spent on research on social problems in organizations had not had the expected results. Since that time, therefore, the authorities and managers have been more cautious in supporting such research and industry's demand for work psychologists has become much less spectacular than it was some years ago. The latter are also now in competition with other specialists and cannot claim monopoly of the field.

B.   Position and status of work psychologists

Currently there are about 600 work psychologists employed in some 300 different organizations. Of these, some 50 work alone and the others are working in small two-to-three member groups. The majority of them are young and a high proportion of them are women. Because of these structural and social factors, the potential of industrial psychologists is not used efficiently as there is no synergic effect.

Individual psychologists can accomplish only fragmentary research and they are too few in number to construct sophisticated research instruments. From the point of view of status, their position in business organizations remains lower than that of engineers and economists. Compared with other specialists, relatively few psychologists achieve leading positions and they are able to impose their point of view less frequently in cooperative, interdisciplinary groups. About half the industrial psychological laboratories are supervised by the head of the personnel department, some 15% by general managers and the rest come under various other staff units.

Some progress has been made in efforts to regulate the legal status of psychologists in industry, but this is still not entirely clarified. Government Act number 250/73 on personnel services in business organizations defines the position and principal functions of the "laboratories of social analysis". According to this Act, the people employed in these laboratories should have psychological or sociological university training at Master's degree level. However, owing to a lack of interest in work psychology on the part of both employers and students alike, this recommendation is by no means universally observed. Training in psychology to the level of Master's degree takes a minimum of four to five years and, although there are four universities with psychology departments teaching industrial and work psychology, the staff specializing in this subject are, in terms of qualifications and experience, very few compared with those dealing with other areas of psychology.

Several ministries, e.g. Ministry of Mining, Ministry of Administration and Environment, Ministry of Transport, Ministry of Chemical Industry, have regulated the status of psychologists in their industry by requiring that people and jobs are subject to psychological assessment, particularly in relation to the prevention of accidents. Thus the Ministry of Transport is responsible for the psychological examination of drivers. The Institute of Transport is in charge of the training of psychologists for testing drivers and it is also entitled to authorize psychological laboratories to carry out such tests.

In a few instances, psychologists who are employed in institutes run by ministries and those holding senior positions in management are engaged in solving problems of personnel policy for a whole branch of industry. They participate, for example, in designing information systems, management development and appraisal schemes, which can be formalized and which may function in several sectors of the national economy. A few psychologists, therefore, have a real influence on policy and strategy, but this is largely as a result of their individual reputations rather than because of their psychological qualifications.

C. Practitioners' clubs

A unique feature of the Polish situation is an informal type of professional association represented by the so-called "Clubs of the Knowledge of Human Work". The first ones were started in 1974 and by 1979 there were forty such clubs spread throughout the important industrial centres of the country. They are sponsored by the trade unions and intended for all behavioural scientists working within industry. Work psychologists, however, predominate among the membership, e.g. constituting over 90% of the Warsaw club, one of the largest and most active. Taken overall, these clubs bring together almost all Polish work psychologists.

The clubs execute two kinds of functions. One is connected with professional affairs, such as the integration of behavioural science practitioners, exchange of experiences and research tools, enlargement and deepening of professional knowledge, and providing an employment service for members. The second concerns practical research and interventions. Although often now preoccupied with logistic rather than human problems, managers' requests for help with the latter remain important. On the initiatives of trade unions and party representatives, clubs are invited by industrial organizations to provide psychological services. Some examples of action research and the problems tackled by club members are as follows:

a. the social activity of employees, their participation in management;
b. functioning of personnel services in business organizations;
c. middle management training in behavioural sciences;
d. individual and group consultancy to foremen;
e. interventions to solve human problems raised in organizations.

In an effort to achieve concrete results, clubs are now tending to concentrate on carefully selected organizations which do not employ behavioural scientists. Psychologists, cooperating with the trade unions, work for these organizations on the basis of systematic development programmes: from diagnosis as the first step to assessment of the effects of the implemented programme. These programmes relate, *inter alia*, to changing employee attitudes by means of educational processes, the quality of working life and work quality improvement, and the foremen's strengthening of authority and leadership.

The organization of these clubs of practitioners is very informal. People usually attend by invitation, but there is no formal method of joining or membership and everyone can come to the club meetings. An executive committee, elected by the members, coordinates their activities. Participation in a club strengthens the psychologist's role *vis-à-vis* his employer, particularly if the psychologist encounters obstacles in research or in the implementation of results, because the clubs can exert influence on employers through the trade union and party officials. It also provides up-to-date information on the problems which the latter groups consider important and thereby brings the activity of work psychologists closer to real life concerns and actual social needs.

D.   Current trends

In terms of the subjects of papers presented by psychologists during the last three years at scientific meetings and conventions of the Polish Psychological Association and symposia organized by the Polish Academy of Sciences, it would seem that Polish industrial psychologists are conducting research mainly in the areas of ergonomics, motivation and social psychology. Papers on employee selection appear only occasionally, although the traditional activities of vocational testing and counselling are still undertaken by most work psychologists.

Some information on the content of industrial psychologists' jobs comes from two surveys, one done in 1973 by the Ministry of Work and Social Welfare and the other in 1976 by the Polish Academy of Science. These showed that, although testing for selection and vocational guidance remain the most frequent activities, they show a tendency to decline. Ergonomic research, including accident prevention, on the other hand, is rapidly expanding, and a third area of development is applied social psychology, e.g. group dynamics, sensitivity training.

Within Polish industry there is a cadre of over 600 psychologists, growing by 10% per year, the majority of them young, well trained in psychological theories and methods, knowing foreign languages, ambitious and proud of their profession. Their potential for dealing with the human problems of industry is great, but, at present, it is not being properly deployed, as the work psychologists are dispersed and submerged within large organizations, often forced to accept tasks not adjusted to their skills. This cadre of work psychologists lacks the leadership which could fight for their proper position in society, willing to launch an attractive programme to develop the profession and knowing how to demonstrate the application of psychology to new areas of economic organizations within the Polish setting.

As a result, and because Polish industrial psychologists are under the pressure of competition from sociologists, economists, organization theorists and even from lawyers, most of whom are trying to apply uncritically behavioural science techniques "discovered" by them in America, some psychologists take refuge in areas to which laymen have no easy access, e.g. ergonomics, testing for vocational guidance, individual counselling and patterns of motivation. Those who are not afraid to approach real life problems and who are prepared to ignore the traditional boundaries of academic disciplines are involved in programmes related to management and organization development, quality of working life and also in some forms of bureaucratic initiative, e.g. personnel record systems, job descriptions, personnel assessment schemes and so on. An essential part of psychologists' influence on management is training managers in the behavioural sciences. The demand for knowledge in this field is enormous as managers are recruited mainly among engineers and have no training in psychology and sociology.

At the start of the 1980s, the uncertainties of the total social and economic situation make it difficult to predict the pattern of Polish work psychology in this decade. Whereas, in 1976, for every newly qualified work psychologist there were ten positions available, the labour market is no longer so spectacular, although not yet menaced by unemployment. On the one hand, there are encouraging signs of interest and support from certain power centres and, on the other, a tendency by managers to regard the claims of behavioural science research as exaggerated. The human potential of Polish work psychology is promising, but there is a lack of adequate leadership and invasion of the field by other specialists. If the existing human problems in industry and the cadre of work psychologists competent in solving these problems can be brought together effectively, a new level of development in Polish work psychology will be reached during the next 2–3 years.

7 Psychological Ergonomics in France

JEAN-CLAUDE SPERANDIO

A. Situation of psychologists in French ergonomics

Ergonomics is not really a well-defined and autonomous profession. However, the practice is increasing whereby psychologists, physiologists and physicians are introducing themselves as ergonomists as a way of labelling their specialization in their own disciplines.

In 1962 the Société d'Ergonomie de Langue Française (French-speaking society of ergonomics), or S.E.L.F. was founded in France. It is affiliated to the International Ergonomics Association (IEA). This academic society has now some 350 members, including 25% foreigners, i.e. French-speaking people from Belgium, Switzerland, Luxembourg, Canada and East Europe. It is difficult to estimate the number of professional ergonomists in the Society — perhaps about 100. Like many professions, ergonomics is not protected by law. Any person, whether or not having graduated in ergonomics, is allowed to practise — and even sometimes to teach — in this field. Thus, the following data have to be interpreted with caution.

About 25% of the members of SELF are psychologists, 60% are physiologists or physicians, the others are mainly engineers, technicians, with some sociologists, economists, and architects. An inquiry by J. M. Faverge (1976) into the membership of the society gives the following figures: 44% are researchers, 34% are employees in an enterprise; 69% say they practise ergonomics in the field, and 48% in the laboratory; 50% believe that ergonomics is primarily a science, against 50% who believe it is a practice. For 62%, ergonomics consists of the application of scientific data, against 38% who believe it is an autonomous applied science; 69% have the opinion that ergonomics will progress through implementation by multidisciplinary teams in the field, rather than through laboratory research. On the one hand, 61% believe that the ergonomist has to provide norms to the design engineer while, on the other, 39% consider that the ergonomist has nothing to do with norms and recipes. Finally, 58% believe that ergonomics is not independent of the social and political context and, indeed, 60% consider that the ergonomist could be an expert in some social conflicts.

As a conclusion to this inquiry, J. M. Faverge observes:

On average, ergonomists are not very influenced by their basic training; thus the SELF succeeds in blending under the label "ergonomics" people of diverse origins. Only psychologists show some characteristics which make them different from the others. Industrial physicians, physiologists, engineers, mainly view ergonomics as "Human engineering", but the physiologists and engineers consider it mainly as a social technology, while physicians see it as engineering with no connection with social problems. Psychologists, for their part, look at ergonomics as a social science consisting of a body of knowledge to be used in the service of the worker.

B.   Research themes

In France, the large-scale development of ergonomics occurred only many years after the end of World War II, mainly in the civil sector (although there are nevertheless important military applications, particularly in the medico-physiological area).

At the beginning of the fifties, psychologists interested in ergonomics focused mainly on work analysis, from the point of view of diagnosing malfunctioning of man–machine systems where the human operator is mainly engaged in information processing. The publication of the book of Ombredane and Faverge (1955) was a milestone in this domain. Although information theory applied to man–machine systems ultimately was not as useful as expected, it was very important at this time, shaping the terminology which is still used, and focusing attention on cognitive processes, which were studied during that period. From the sixties onwards, the development of large-scale automated processes has provided ergonomics with the opportunity to study the interface between the logic of information-processing by computers and the logic of information-processing by operators. This led some psychologists to conduct researches directly in the field, drawing upon results of researches in fundamental psychology, but elaborating genuine problematics. Systematization of the different stages of information processing concerning the task and the operators was made possible through borrowing the flow charts of computer science to formalize the reasoning processes involved.

A typical example of this type of ergonomics was the study of Air Traffic Control, mainly by a team located at the Institut de Recherches d'Information et d'Automatisme (Roquencourt). Level of initial training, mental load, variations in the strategies of the operators were the more important variables. More generally, there are now in France many groups of psychologists studying different aspects of cognitive ergonomics in relation to the automation of tasks, for example the human interactions with the "terminals". Formalization of reasoning, mental representation of the working system, perception, storage and retrieval of information, constitute some of the most frequent themes of research.

"Cognitive ergonomics" is not limited to automated tasks. There is also, for instance in the Laboratoire de Psychologie du Travail in Paris, general research on codification in verbal and non-verbal communications, mental load and so on. In relation to road safety, a laboratory (ONSER, Monthléry) is studying the behaviour and attitudes of drivers. At the Institut National de Recherches sur la Sécurité (Nancy), there is a group of psychologists working on problems related to accidents in industry.

Another feature of the evolution of psychological ergonomics is that psychosocial variables are increasingly taken into account. Notably, there is a growing interest in what is described by a relatively vague and ambiguous term "amelioration of the conditions of work" (something like "quality of working life"). Due to the social and political significance of this topic, psychologists in ergonomics are called upon increasingly to undertake research and to make interventions in this domain, particularly concerning the so-called "new forms of work organization" such as job enrichment, autonomous groups. There are also some interesting attempts to study influence of working life on non-working life (mainly for women workers).

In France, ergonomics is no longer limited to the traditional area of industry. There are some recent studies which have been done in offices, hospitals, schools, agriculture, and in the design of buildings, the latter in association with architects.

C. Training in psychological ergonomics

There are no specific training courses leading to a degree in ergonomics, but the subject may be approached from many different backgrounds, particularly at the undergraduate level. Psychological ergonomics is taught as a part of work psychology, but it may also be taken in parallel with physiological ergonomics.

At the doctorate level, there are about 12 universities where psychological ergonomics is taught in the context of work psychology; in one of them psychological ergonomics is the main topic. There is only one official specific course in ergonomics, which naturally includes psychological ergonomics.

The place of psychological ergonomics in the academic curriculum is approximately in proportion to the professional opportunities available to graduate students. But extensive effort is needed to make managers (in both the private and public sectors) familiar with this aspect of ergonomics. Industrial ergonomics, indeed, is still associated with the traditional image of the industrial medical officer or of the physiologist specializing in physically demanding work. In comparison, the psychologist's image is never that of someone versed in the technical aspects of production systems, but remains that of the specialist in vocational selection and training or in industrial relations. It is therefore vital to change this image so that psychological ergonomics can make its full contribution.

References

FAVERGE, J. M. (1976). L'ergonomie vue pas les ergonomes. *Le Travail Humain*, 39, 299–310.
OMBREDANE, A. AND FAVERGE, J. M. (1955). *L'analyse du Travail*. P.U.F., Paris.

8 Developments in the Domain: The Case of Personnel Selection

CHARLES J. DE WOLFF

A. Introduction

Selection is one of the oldest and most well established areas of work psychology which, in many countries, still forms the major part of the domain. Thus, for many clients, work psychology and personnel selection are more or less synonymous. Psychological textbooks cover the subject extensively and, contrary to the treatment given to other areas, often prescribe in great detail how work psychologists should carry out a personnel selection programme. Furthermore, unlike those parts of the domain which show considerable overlap with other social sciences, selection is the undisputed territory of work psychologists. As a result, psychologists have succeeded in making others who want to work in the selection area look like quacks and bunglers! Even so, work psychologists themselves do not necessarily agree on the subject. Today, as well as in the past, there are conflicts and controversies among scientists, professionals, clients and regulatory bodies about professional practice.

The purpose of this chapter is to discuss these conflicts and contradictions relating to selection and thereby illustrate the themes developed in Section 1. It will be shown that there are differences in definition; that a domain is dynamic and not static; that there is a dominant faction in the profession which shapes the behaviour of members; that there are conflicting ideologies; and that the profession has to respond to a turbulent environment. The situation described refers primarily to developments in the Netherlands, where the author has been active in the domain for over twenty five years in many different roles, e.g. as an author, an editor, a test-constructor, a programme director, and president of a professional association. My observations are based on my own experience as well as the professional literature, but I believe that parallel developments to those described for the Netherlands can be found in other countries.

B.   Clinical versus statistical approaches

Until the late nineteen fifties, the clinical approach to selection prevailed in the Netherlands. A number of companies had introduced psychological selection programmes in the pre-war period and there were a number of institutes offering services to organizations of which some of the larger ones had close associations with universities, e.g. where the director of an institute also held a chair in psychology. As there were very few psychologists at that time it was not uncommon to find most of the selection work done by non-psychologists. German psychologists were influential and German textbooks were well read, with *Verstehende Psychologie* seen as more respectable than *Erklärende Psychologie*. Practitioners used mainly what one would now call an impressionistic approach in which, as Nuttin (1954) put it, a psychologist tried to have a direct and profound human contact with a person in order to give some form of therapy or advice. The emphasis was on direct communication and *einfühlen* (to feel one's way). To facilitate this, observation tests and projective techniques were used (Wiggleyblocks, Rorschach, Baumtest, graphology), but only a few paper and pencil tests suitable for Dutch subjects existed.

Psychologists also stressed the scientific nature of their activities calling their institutes laboratories, their clients subjects and their associate staff assistants. They studied the intellectual qualities of their subjects, their temperament and character, and wrote lengthy reports about them. The amount of time involved in assessing someone often approached two days and the resulting report might easily exceed 1000–1500 words, its quality depending more on the attributes of the psychologist (or his senior assistant) and less on his educational qualifications. Intuition was more important than training, although it was clear that certain qualities had to be cultivated. Much of what had been done in Anglo-Saxon countries was little known to Dutch students. During my own training, which was from 1947 to 1953, the major part of the programme was devoted to philosophy and it was mainly through my first job in the selection centre of the Dutch Royal Navy that I became acquainted with the work of psychologists like Guilford (1949), Thorndike (1949) and Vernon (1949).

Psychological testing had been adopted by the Dutch Navy at the end of World War II using a test battery developed for the British Navy and adapted by some Dutch officers. After the war, one of these officers got permission to study psychology, simultaneously with his regular work, and was the first psychologist employed by the Navy. The resulting situation offered splendid opportunities to young psychologists to familiarize themselves with all kinds of selection methods. One could experiment with different tests and try out all kinds of approaches described in the literature. Another important factor was that the Navy received copies of various reports from the American military forces and had books available like the *Army Air Forces Aviation Psychology Research Program* (1947) and *The American Soldier* (Stouffer, 1949). In this setting, it did not take long to become convinced of the "superiority" of the statistical approach.

At the end of the fifties a dramatic change occurred. By then a second generation of psychologists had come into existence and almost every university had one psychology professor, who had been a pioneer in the field. In this second generation there were a number of psychologists who were clearly devoted to the statistical approach and so the prevailing orientation altered. The change can be seen in the contents of the Dutch journal *Netherlands Tijdschrift voor de Psychologie* for that period. In 1957, van Lennep, writing as one who had himself made an important contribution to the development of projective techniques and who was then director of one of the largest selection institutes, holding a chair of psychology at Utrecht, commented: "Basically, projective tests do not satisfy the demands which have to be made to have predictive value and one should draw the consequences from this."

This new direction came at an important moment, when university departments were beginning to expand and new professors had to be appointed. A new and different dominant faction emerged, greatly influenced by American psychologists. American books were widely read, Dutch psychologists visited the United States, and American professors were invited to lecture at Dutch universities. Although the change was not restricted to work psychology, but occurred throughout the subject, selection occupied a central position. In 1957, 15% of psychologists described themselves as work psychologists, and 24% as generalists. Of the latter, many were engaged in selection work for at least part of their time. Furthermore, clinical psychologists (15%) and child psychologists (18%) were mainly occupied with psycho-diagnostic work (Krijnen, 1975). So the "clinical" versus "statistical" issue was central to almost all psychologists.

As a consequence of these changes, new activities were started, e.g. the professional association set up a test research and development committee and established a research division which was intended to stimulate communication between all psychologists using statistical methods. Training programmes also changed, and students were now taught to use the new approach. Thus in a relatively short period there was a reorientation and a redefinition of problems leading to different kinds of activity. Selection was no longer seen as a matter of profound human contact, but as an issue of measuring human properties. It was no longer regarded as an individual appraising a subject, but as a procedure relating predictors to criteria, e.g. ". . . the reputable worker in the field is continuously concerned with testing verifying and improving the adequacy of his procedures" (Thorndike, 1949). The new approach was certainly very prescriptive and clearly distinguished between good and bad practice, Thorndike observing that "A personnel selection program which does not involve empirical checks of the selection procedures against criteria of job success is at best a static and untested one. At worst it might be outright charlatanism."

However, although the prevailing ideology changed, practice changed much less. Many practitioners who were accustomed to using projective techniques and observation tests continued to do so and even now, twenty years later, these kinds of tests are still used, and in many cases, selection advice is not based on validated programmes. Often the introduction of new test batteries met with resistance from practitioners, who liked to keep what they had used before and found difficulties in having to replace known, but no longer reputable, methods by more respectable, but less familiar ones. Some surveys amongst Dutch test users show that projective techniques are still widely used. Evers and Zaal (1979), who collected their data in 1976, conclude that the use of outdated tests, which are not or are insufficiently validated, is still rather common. Comparing their data with those from two earlier surveys, they also show that there has not been much improvement, even though more than half of the test users in their new sample had graduated after 1971 and were supposed to have been properly trained in selection methods at their universities. Such findings give reason for concern. Although one can blame practitioners and attribute their behaviour to stubbornness, ignorance, or any other unfavourable personality trait, that will not lead to a solution. One has to realize that the statistical approaches only partly meet the problems confronting practitioners who have to work with small samples, with groups which are not homogeneous and who lack adequate criteria. In these circumstances it is difficult to get resources for validation studies, especially when clients like to have a detailed report about the individual applicants. There may also be weaknesses in the "statistical approach" itself and these too may have to be remedied.

C.   Prediction

Psychologists like Thorndike (1949) saw selection primarily as a prediction problem; they wanted to foretell future performance of applicants. In principle any property of a subject could be used to predict this, but, in practice, intellectual capabilities and personality traits got the most attention. This approach had been very successful during World War II, when large numbers of conscripts had to be allocated and when the pilot selection programme, in particular, had yielded spectacular results. So it was assumed that selection programmes could be very useful in peacetime in industry, in educational systems, and in other organizations. Basically, selection was a set of procedures, which had to be executed properly, and one might say that during the forties and fifties a selection technology had been developed. Textbooks like Thorndike's described how to apply such a technology. There were also methods for test construction, factor analysis, etc. The interest was primarily in measurement, that is a subject was a system with properties, for which one should find appropriate constructs and measure these in a suitable way.

Implicit in this approach were some assumptions about human behaviour. The first was that performance is dependent on individual differences and so much attention was given to the study of traits. Later there was surprise when it was discovered that the multiple correlations obtained were usually low, so that some psychologists even talked about a "ceiling" (Rundquist, 1969).

The second assumption concerned definition of the criterion. The statistical approach assumes that criteria can be measured and that it is possible to define in advance a person's contribution to the organization. This, according to Thorndike (1949) was the ultimate criterion, "the complete final goal of a particular type of selection". Later, when organizations were seen as "open systems", operating in a "turbulent environment", such an assumption about "complete final goals" lost something of its credibility.

A third assumption had to do with the labour market. Selection presumes that there are more applicants than vacancies. However, in the post-war period in the Netherlands, the labour reserve was low, for most of the time below 1%. Even now when it is over 5%, there are still categories of jobs for which it is difficult to recruit workers. Seen from the prediction point of view one should not use selection procedures with unfavourable selection ratios but, in spite of this, many companies continued to use psychological testing programmes.

A fourth implicit assumption was that the psychological testing programme could be isolated from all other activities in the organization. Psychologists administered their tests, preferably in their laboratories, wrote their reports, and reported to management. The procedures were not seen as affecting the applicants in any way, e.g. they were not supposed to influence willingness to work for the organization, motivation or future performance. This does not mean that there were no other views on the subject or that psychologists working on other problems, such as human factor studies and leadership problems, were not using quite different assumptions, e.g. that performance is dependent on the technical system or on interactions between individuals. A glance at older issues of journals reveals statements which were ignored at the time (e.g. in 1950 Bingham condensed his views in the question: "Persons or guineapigs?"). But the main stream was moving in other directions, so it happened that problems which were spotted very early by some, only became pressing later.

D. Fairness

Psychologists' views on selection were seriously questioned during the nineteen sixties and seventies. This started in the United States, where books like *The Brain Watchers* (Gross, 1962), *The Tiranny of Testing* (Hoffman, 1962) and *The Naked Society* (Packard, 1964) fiercely attacked psychological selection procedures. Psychologists had to defend their practices during hearings by special committees of the United States Senate and House of Representatives (the *American Psychologist*, November, 1965). At first the discussion concentrated on the "invasion of privacy" but later, "discrimination" became the main issue when the United States government sought to promote the emancipation of minorities through legislation, and to prevent forms of discrimination against these groups. "Equal employment opportunities" then became the catchphrase. The chapters devoted to personnel selection in the *Annual Review of Psychology* show this clearly. In the 1969 issue, the subject gets little attention, but in 1972 Bray and Moses state that the test fairness controversy predominates, while in 1975 Ash and Kroecke observe that psychologists are more and more involved in legal issues.

In the Netherlands there was extensive discussion amongst psychologists, particularly in the second part of the sixties, about privacy (Van Strien, 1966; Drenth, 1967) and later about the role of the psychologist and the position of the applicant (see Van Strien, 1976). In 1971 questions were put in the Dutch Parliament to the Minister of Social Affairs and in 1973 an institute established by the unions published a study taking a critical view of prevailing selection policies. The gist of the objections was that applicants find themselves in a difficult position when they apply for a job. It was argued that, when the organization has well-organized procedures employing different sorts of professionals to assess applicants, the latter are placed at a disadvantage. So a plea was made to strengthen the position of the applicant to enable him to meet the organization on a more equal basis. This criticism coincided with a wider discussion, in which organizations were seen as having a negative impact on the well-being of workers because they were governed by "economic" rather than "social" principles. Work psychologists providing services to organizations were asked to declare their loyalties, e.g. if they subscribed to organizational values, assisting organizations to make a larger profit, or if they sought to serve the interests of individual workers.

In 1973 the Minister of Social Affairs established a committee to study recruitment and selection practices, particularly to see if it was desirable to protect the personal interests of workers. This was a difficult assignment and it took the committee four years to prepare a final report (Hessel, 1977) in which a legalistic approach is clearly discernible. The committee adopted two principles: firstly, the criterion for selection should be fitness for a job, and secondly that all parts of the total selection procedure should be in accordance with human dignity.

These were expanded in a number of rights:

a. to a fair chance of appointment, i.e. decisions should be seriously considered based on fair arguments, and should always be justifiable;

b. to information, i.e. both parties involved in a selection procedure should get the necessary information for making a justifiable decision;

c. to privacy, i.e. recognition that an applicant has to provide some information about himself, but only information relevant to the position should be elicited;

d. to confidential treatment of information;

e. to the use of effective procedures, i.e. selection instruments should be valid and reliable;

f. the right of appeal.

Jansen (1979), who was a member of the committee, has published a book on selection which is clearly prescriptive describing how a "fair procedure" should be carried out.

To some extent, the Netherlands Institute of Psychologists (the Dutch Professional Association) had anticipated these developments. In 1970 it established a committee to prepare a revision of the code of conduct. After extensive discussions a new code was accepted in 1975 dealing, among other issues, with confidentiality and appeal procedures. It also states that subjects can insist that psychologists do not report on them to management (NIP, 1976).

E.   Mutual interests

During the seventies another view on selection emerged. This sees selection and placement as a process of negotiating a psychological contract between an organization, on the one hand, trying to find an employee who can meet certain job demands and, on the other, an applicant looking for a job through which he or she can satisfy certain needs. Several American authors subscribe to this view. Thus Lofquist and Dawis (1969) describe a model in which there are two adjustment processes, one between workers' abilities and job demands, leading to satisfactoriness, the other between workers' needs and organizational rewards, leading to satisfaction. Lofquist and Dawis stress that adjustment is a continuous process, i.e. that both the individual and the organization have to work constantly to achieve an equilibrium.

Another example can be found in the Agent Selection Kit developed by the Life Insurance Agency Management Association in the early seventies. In a mimeographed manual for this kit it is emphasized that procedures should be integrated and that selection should be seen as part of a manpower development programme. Furthermore, decisions should rest on "mutual consent" and both parties should take part in "mutual exploration". Although each of these concepts would merit further discussion, I will abstain from it here. For present purposes it is sufficient to note that a number of concepts are used which are quite different from those used in earlier, more traditional studies. For example, it is remarkable how differently interviews are treated in this kit. The Association has done extensive research on selection interviews (Mayfield and Carlson, 1966). When prediction was stressed, psychologists were rather suspicious about interviews as it was felt that conclusions based on them usually impaired the predictive power of selection procedures. Some psychologists even considered skipping the interview altogether! In the "mutual interest" approach, however, interviews are given a much more central position, especially for establishing a psychological contract. Likewise, mutual exploration can only be achieved in this way.

Schneider (1977) also emphasizes that there are two parties involved in selection processes and that selection cannot be seen as an isolated activity. An integrated approach is needed to processes such as identifying, assessing, evaluating and developing individuals' potential at work. Similarly, in the Netherlands, de Wolff and van den Bosch (1980) underline the need for an integrated approach, stressing that there are two decision-making processes, one by the organization and the other by the individual. Selection procedures ought to facilitate both processes and the psychologist assist both parties. Such a view leads to a new set of research questions, e.g. what needs does an individual try to satisfy in work, how can these be assessed during the selection procedure, what kinds of information are applicants interested in, how should this be presented, and so on. It also suggests that attainments in some other parts of the domain, such as motivation studies, leadership studies, etc. may be used to approach selection problems more adequately.

Dunnette and Borman (1979), in the Annual Review, see a broader approach due to the many separate lines of influence and discovery. They strike an optimistic note, observing that "we look towards the next few years as a time when personnel selection can take rapid strides to assure improved matches between persons and jobs for the good of everyone". They also see an opportunity "to satisfy more fully the needs of both organizations and individuals". A major value expressed in their review is the conservation of human talent and they end their chapter with the hope that "selection will contribute to the optimal utilization of human resources for the total economy". Such an expression would not be used by most European psychologists, who would be more likely to take a more humanistic stance.

In this chapter, I have tried to demonstrate that selection problems can be seen in quite different ways. There are different problem definitions depending on beliefs, views and ideologies or, if one prefers a different wording, there are different paradigms. Accepting a certain definition inevitably leads to a channelling of activities, e.g. the prediction approach drew attention to measurement problems. The social context is also important. Psychologists are influenced by others and they exert influence through their publications and professional contacts. They are affected by leading ideologies in our society and it is likely that major events have an impact, e.g. Dunnette and Borman note the great advances in personnel assessment which have occurred during periods of crisis (the two world wars). It is clear that the domain is not fixed, but that it is dynamic. There are constant activities by psychologists and others which shape the domain and from time to time lead to its extensive restructuring.

Examples have also been given of the dominant faction influencing the behaviour of members by emphasizing important values (Katz and Kahn, 1978). In publications one can find many expressions which act like flags, pointing out the orientation of the author (e.g. "conservation of human resources", "mutual consent", "a fair chance of appointment", *Verstehende Psychologie*). Even in approaches that look scientific, values are involved (e.g. a test battery predicting a certain criterion with a correlation coefficient of 0·50 is "better" than one of 0·40). Currently, different values are shown in the different emphases given to "contributions to the total economy", "growth opportunities for individuals", "right to self-determination" and "equal employment opportunities". Thus it is clear that professionals operate in a "turbulent" environment.

Overall, I tend to share Dunnette's and Borman's optimistic feelings. As a result of the enormous amount of research, not only on selection problems but also on all kinds of behaviour in organizations, psychologists have acquired extensive knowledge and insight which can be used to structure selection procedures. In this sense there has certainly been great advance in the past decades so the claim of psychologists that they, as professionals, can make important contributions to the solution of selection problems is warranted. Nevertheless, the substantiation of this claim require much effort, not only scientifically but also in organizational terms in the relationship with clients, government bodies, with other disciplines and the general public.

References

ARMY AIR FORCES AVIATION PSYCHOLOGY RESEARCH PROGRAM REPORTS (1947). Government Printing Office, Washington.

ASH, P. AND KROECKER, L. P. (1975). Personnel selection, classification and placement. *Annual Review of Psychology* 26, 481–508.

BINGHAM, W. V. (1950). Persons or guinea pigs? *Personnel Psychology*, 3, 305–400.

BRAY, D. W. AND MOSES, J. L. (1972). Personnel selection. *Annual Review of Psychology*, 23, 545–576.

DE WOLFF, Ch. J. AND VAN DER BOSCH, G. Personeelsaanname. In *Handboek Arbeids- en Organisatiepsychologie*. Van Loghum Slaterus, Deventer. (Forthcoming.)

DRENTH, P. J. D. (1967). *Protesten Contra Testen.* Swets & Zeitlinger, Amsterdam.

DUNNETTE, M. D. AND BORMAN, W. C. (1979). Personnel selection and classification system. *Annual Review of Psychology*, 30, 477–526.

EVERS, A. AND ZAAL, J. (1979). De derde N.I.P.-enquête onder testgebruikers. *De psycholoog*, **XIV**, blz. 509-528.

GROSS, M. L. (1962). *The Brain Watchers*. Random House, New York.

GUILFORD, J. P. AND LACEY, J. I. (eds) (1947). *Printed Classification Tests*. Army Air Forces Aviation Psychology Research Program Reports, Report 5. U.S. Government Printing Office, Washington.

HESSEL, commissie. (1977). *Een Sollicitant is ook een Mens*. Sociale Zaken, Staatsuitgeverij, 's-Gravenhage.

HOFFMAN, B. (1962). *The Tiranny of Testing* . Crowell, Collier, New York.

JANSEN, A. (1979). *Ethiek en Praktijk van Personeelsselectie*. Kluwer, Deventer.

KATZ, D. AND KAHN, R. L. (1978). *The Psychology of Organizations* (2nd edition). John Wiley, New York.

KRIJNEN, G. (1975). *Ontwikkeling Functievervulling van Psychologen*, deel I. Instituut voor Toegepaste Psychologie, Nijmegen.

KRIJNEN, G. (1976). *Ontwikkeling Functievervulling van Psychologen*, deel II, Institut voor Toegepaste Psychologie, Nijmegen.

LIAMA (1968). *Agent Selection Kit*. Hartford.

LOFQUIST, L. H. AND DAWIS, R. V. (1969). *Adjustment to Work*. Appleton-Century-Crofts, New York.

MAYFIELD, E. C. (1964). The selection interview: A reevaluation of published research. *Personnel Psychology*, **17**, 239-260.

MAYFIELD, E. C. AND CARLSON, R. E. (1966). Selection interview decisions: First results from longterm research project. *Personnel Psychology*, **19**, 41-53.

NEDERLANDS INSTITUUT VAN PSYCHOLOGEN (1975). Beroepscode voor psychologen. *De Psycholoog*, **10**, 279-285.

NUTTIN, J. (1954). Clinische en experimentele methoden in de psychologie, *Nederlands Tijdschrift voor de Psychologie*, **IX**, 97-113.

PACKARD, V. (1964). *The Naked Society*. McKay, New York.

RUNDQUIST, E. A. (1969). The prediction ceiling. *Personnel Psychology*, **22**, 109-116.

SCHNEIDER, B. (1976). *Staffing Organizations*. Goodyear Publishing Company. Pacific Palisades.

STICHTING WETENSCHAPPELIJK ONDERZOEK VAKCENTRALES (1973). *De Afhanklijke Sollicitant*. Lumax, Utrecht.

STOUFFER, S. A. (1949). *The American Soldier*. Princeton University Press, New York.

THORNDIKE, L. J. (1949). *Personnel Selection, Test and Measurement Technique*. John Wiley, New York.

VAN LENNEP, D. J. (1957). de ontwikkeling van het testonderzoek in de bedrijfspsychologie. *Nederlands Tijdschrift voor de Psychologie*. **XII**, 270-277.

VAN STRIEN, P. J. (1966). *Kennis en Communicatie in de Psychologische Praktijk*. Bijleveld, Utrecht.

VAN STRIEN, P. J. (ed.) (1976). *Personeelsselectie in Discussie*. Boom, Meppel.

VERNON, P. E. AND PARRY, J. B. (1949). *Personnel Selection in the British Forces*. University of London Press, London.

9 Working Life in Sweden in the 1990s

GÖRAN EKVALL

A. Introduction

What decides our future working life? Is it the supply of energy and raw materials? Is it technological breakthroughs and innovations? Is it global economic and trade policy conditions? Or is it philosophic currents, ideologies, values, "political will" and such intellectual rather than material matters that are decisive?

It is, of course, preposterous to frame the question like that. Just as preposterous as to ask what comes first: material changes or changes of ideas. It is obvious that changes of material conditions have an effect on peoples' attitudes, values and ideas. And it is equally obvious that ideas can remove mountains. Material changes will occur and they will influence our working life. These are realities which we cannot disregard. The energy problems exist and so do the ecological problems and so forth, and they will be given solutions of some sort. But what these solutions will be is, to a great extent, dependent on political and ideological values and judgements. The debate on energy policy that is going on all over the world shows this very clearly. This is not merely a judgement of technical and economic advantages and disadvantages of different energy sources. To a great degree, it is about what the social structure of the future society will be like.

A more reasonable way to frame the question would be to ask what ideas will interact with what material conditions and changes in how these will influence working life in the future. As a consequence, research on the future must be interdisciplinary. Contributions must come from scientists of various kinds: from technologists and economists as well as from historians of ideas, philosophers, psychologists, sociologists and political scientists. It is significant that the large institutes for research on the future which exist in the United States, as well as in Europe, have an enormous scope as regards the scientific background and location of their staff members. It is also significant that many of the authors who have written important popular scientific books on the subject are not scientists themselves, but journalists with a great intellectual breadth and receptivity who have been capable of compiling and integrating research results from widely differing fields.

Another consequence of the view that material factors, as well as ideas, determine the future is that different outcomes are predicted according to whether or not a materialistic determinism is taken as the starting point. If, in fact, ideas can influence the future, then there is every reason for creating alternatives and trying to control the development by means of these alternatives. If, on the other hand, the development is, to a great extent, ruled by unyielding conformity to law, the sole purpose of research on the future would be to prepare people for what is coming.

The unpretentious studies on future working life in Sweden, on which this article is based, have a clear inclination towards the side that has to do with ideas. We have principally been interested in those philosophies about working life and its goals from which one may expect an effect on development. This means that we have concentrated on social and psychological matters like work motivation, work organization, co-determination, personnel policy goals, etc., as it is through such concepts that these philosophies are implemented. We have not been primarily interested in prognoses about energy consumption, technical development of industrial robots, distribution of labour between the various branches, the future of the export industry, the raw material situation of the country, and other materialistic variables which have an influence on the future state of working life. We have restricted ourselves in this way, partly due to financial and time constraints and partly because we would like to believe that ideologies, political goals, democratic decisions will be the principal elements steering the future.

The procedure applied in our studies was to ask competent people what they thought of future working life. We have not done any opinion polls and asked the man in the street about his view of the future. That kind of research has, of course, its importance too; but it was not our target. Instead, we approached people whom we expected to be good judges of present working life conditions and problems and who were also likely to have thought about future trends.

Three studies have been carried out. In the first one, sixty staff managers and consultants in the field of personnel administration participated. A questionnaire method was applied. In the second and third studies we used a variation of the scenario method.

In the second study, we approached a group whom we considered to be experts on the development of working life. The group consisted of researchers specializing on today's working life and researchers specializing on future working life, as well as of consultants engaged in long-term planning in companies and authors who have written about society in the future.

The third study concerned a group of people who were neither experts, nor representative of the man in the street. It was a group of high-grade, municipal officials whom we asked to compare the future they would wish for and the future they expected.

What follows is based on the results of these studies, presenting a free description of three different lines of development in Sweden which could be seen from the results.

B.   Three scenarios

Prognoses of the development of the labour market in the USA predict a dramatic decline in the number of industrial employees during the next decades as a consequence of new techniques involving the use of computers and robots. The decline will affect manufacturing jobs as well as engineering and administrative jobs. According to a survey made by the public opinion institute Testologen, many industrialists and computer experts believe that we shall have a similar trend in Sweden. Labour forecasts made by the Central Bureau of Statistics suggest, however, much less dramatic changes. It is true that industrial work is expected to employ a smaller part of the labour force in 1990 than it did in 1975 (27% against 32%) but, in absolute figures, there will be no decline, as the total number of gainfully employed individuals is expected to increase. And the share of engineering and administrative jobs is expected to remain unchanged. The only considerable decline in relative, as well as in absolute, terms predicted by the Central Bureau of Statistics concerns agricultural and forest work. The big increases will occur in medical and other service work. These are the sectors of the labour market which will absorb the increase in the labour force as a whole as well as redundant labour from other areas.

A good half of the "experts on future" (8 out of 15) engaged in our study were of the opinion that working life is in the process of automation and computerization, in line with the more dramatic forecasts. The other half of the "experts" (7 out of 15) considered quite another development more likely, namely that production will be mostly manual and take place in small units, with considerable decentralization of decisions.

The future which emerged as a result of projecting the economic, political and technological lines of development which have dominated the Western world ever since the breakthrough of industrialism was more or less as would be expected. Eight of our fifteen expert judges believe that these tendencies will continue, whereas the other seven experts apparently think that we shall have to face rather abrupt changes. All agreed, however, that working life will be characterized by extensive employee influence and a philosophy of self-realization.

The group of high-grade municipal officials anticipated large-scale, automated production. Unlike the afore-mentioned expert judges, they are not optimistic about the chances of self-realization for the employees. They are also less optimistic than the experts with regard to increased participation. Instead, they believe that people will adopt an instrumental attitude to work and seek satisfaction of their needs in their leisure time. But they find the trend they forecast undesirable. Likewise, in our first study, the managers and consultants in personnel administration predicted a more inhuman future than the one considered likely by the expert judges.

In the light of these findings, as well as those of other future studies, we have outlined three possible lines of development for working life in Sweden. These differ greatly from one another. But, they have one thing in common, namely, that their contours can be extracted from our own material like puzzle pictures. We have, however, allowed ourselves a great deal of freedom when filling out the pictures.

Scenario I (B.1) can be described as a gentle and humane, large-scale option. Scenario II (B.2) is also a large-scale option, but a hard and materialistic one. Scenario III (B.3) is best described in words like "small-scale production" and "decentralization".

The three pictures presented below are rather absolute. In reality, of course there is no such thing as a single line of development, but it is possible that one rather than another may exert a dominant influence in the nineties.

1. SCENARIO I

The concentration in industrial and commercial life has continued. Industrial production takes place mainly in large, highly automated units. The few people who actually work in the factories are occupied with loading, supervision, repair and maintenance of the machines. Production is organized in such a way as to provide those engaged in it with tasks that are both full of variety and involve responsibility. Small groups of employees are responsible for all tasks around a group of machines. No one is occupied solely with, for instance, loading or supervision. Each group is responsible for planning and control within given production targets. For example, they decide themselves how to schedule preventive maintenance. Even some of the programming work is done by the members of the group, although process routing and primary planning are done centrally by engineers.

Commerce and services are run by big companies and chain stores. Owing to the expansion of the service sector, many former industrial workers have been able to find jobs with these companies. Administration and planning are highly computerized. Sales, on the other hand, mainly take place at a personal level. Repairs are carried out approximately as at present. All tasks are organized so as to prevent monotony and fatigue. For example, no one is solely a cashier in a self-service store, no one is solely washing cars, no one sits at a data terminal all day long. Job rotation, job enlargement and similar methods are applied to give the employees variety and psychological benefit from work.

The social service sector has absorbed a great deal of redundant labour from industry. Large units are also typical of this sector, in which administration is computerized to a large extent. But the trend towards specialization and routinization of medical and other social services, evident during the sixties and seventies, has been abandoned.

The employees are entrusted with enlarged responsibility. Delegation of tasks downwards in the hierarchy has been accomplished. At work, democracy is well developed. Employees and their union representatives have the right of self-determination on many issues concerning both personnel policy and production. Furthermore, the philosophy of working life is characterized by consideration for the individual.

Economic growth and an increased material standard of living is still a dominating political goal which leads to striving for high productivity. But other goals connected with the satisfaction of psychological needs — "quality of working life" — are also given high priority and quite often lead to modification of the demands for productivity. Safety requirements are very strict and seldom or never set aside for the sake of effectiveness.

2. SCENARIO II

The concentration in industry and commerce is far advanced. Practically all production of goods and services is on a large scale. Public administration and services are similarly organized. Automation and computerization have brought about high productivity which is the cardinal goal. But, at the same time, human contacts in working life have diminished both quantitatively and qualitatively.

The specialization of tasks is complete at almost all levels. In factories and offices people sit tied and isolated at control panels and data screens all day long. Qualified specialists carry out advanced but narrow tasks. Production control is centralized; leadership is authoritarian and strict and mainly exercised through messages on data screens. The medical services are also automated, computerized and specialized. Contacts between patients and nursing staff are sparse and formal.

Economic growth is the overshadowing political goal. Efficiency and productivity are given high priority at the expense of other values. Sweden is trying at all costs to keep up with an ever-increasing international competition. Most people accept this tendency and submit to working under stress and monotony in order to maintain or increase their material standard of living. The few industrial jobs are well paid; it is considered good to have such a job, in spite of the fact that it is isolated and dull. Industrial companies can pick and choose their workers from a long queue of applicants. So can the public service institutions, which have taken over many of the redundant industrial workers.

3. SCENARIO III

The days of the large production units are over. Big companies have been decentralized and split up into smaller, independent subsidiary companies. Decentralization is the keyword. Small-scale business is stimulated and extending. Both goods and services are, to a large extent, produced by hand with the aid of flexible, often electric hand-tools and lifting devices. Computers are being used, but these are mainly small and function principally as auxiliary tools. In all sections of the labour market there is an ambition to obstruct specialization and routinization by means of job enlargement, job rotation and joint decision making. Staff and their union representatives have the right to decide many important issues. Working life democracy is far advanced. There is a great flexibility in order to satisfy the individual's needs with respect to tasks, environment, working hours, etc.

The dramatic decrease of industrial jobs depicted in some of today's forecasts has not occurred. Industrial production is work-intensive and energy-saving and therefore provides many jobs. In the retail trade too, the small units are back. Shopping centres exist, but these consist of small, specialized shops of various kinds. In housing areas, there are shops for everyday commodities and small service and repair shops. A great deal of the medical service is carried out in small units within housing areas. This applies, for instance, to long-term treatment, psychiatric care, maternity care and convalescence. Advanced acute treatment, on the other hand, takes place in more specialized units.

Economic and political goals have changed considerably. Economic growth and a rising material standard of living have been abandoned as desirable objectives. Sweden is no longer trying, as she did before, to keep up with international competition. Exports and imports have decreased considerably. Consequently, Sweden has become less dependent on foreign countries. But the material standard of living has gone down. We have fewer cars, TV sets, house trailers, cameras, snack bars, motor boats or luxury furniture than in the seventies. Nor can we make as many trips abroad. But, on the other hand, we have an easier working pace, more pleasant working days, friendlier contacts between people, both in working life and elsewhere, a more wholesome diet, more "family life" through joint activities such as growing plants, doing repair work, gathering berries or mushrooms, building a house and so forth.

Scenario I gives a picture of the future which will probably not arouse any strong emotional reactions, either positive or negative. It seems all too familiar. It is what one might expect to come out of the changes that have been evident during the last decades. This is also apparent from the massive discussion on the working environment, industrial democracy, robotization, computerization, structural changes in the labour market which is taking place in the media and in everyday conversation. It seems likely that people in Sweden expect:

a. that companies will grow bigger and bigger (Volvo and SAAB will merge; the shipyards will become one huge combine; the many steel works will be merged into two or three mammoth companies; there will be more super-markets but the number of chains owning them will be no greater than today);

b. there will be fewer jobs in industry, but, on the other hand, there will be more jobs in services and in the medical sector;

c. jobs in factories and offices will be automated or computerized to a large extent;

d. job rotation, job enlargement, autonomous work groups, decentralization of decisions etc. will make work more stimulating and provide more opportunities for personal growth than today;

e. when work is being planned and organized, great attention will be paid to individual needs, qualifications and interests;

f. the work environment will be good and health and safety requirements will be very strict;

g. employees and their unions will have a great deal of influence — much more than they have today;

h. the present high standard of living will have been maintained, but other values will be operative. This means that a constant rise in the material standard of living is no longer being sought. People are willing to give up profit and pay rises to get better and more pleasant working conditions.

These ideas are not threatening or surprising, but nor do they arouse enthusiasm. The prerequisite for this picture of the future is that Swedish industry and trade can produce and sell goods and services profitably on an international market.

Scenario II describes a picture that most people will find disagreeable and frightening. Possibly, some may be attracted by the "tough struggle and tight reins" aspect but these will probably be those who expect to be holding the reins. To almost anyone, this scenario probably poses the question of how to avoid a future in which,

1. people work like slaves in dreary jobs to be able to consume more and more;
2. work is regarded as a hell that one has to put up with to be able to afford a satisfactory leisure time;
3. in companies, as well as in other workplaces, the greatest influence is in the hands of a few experts;
4. a bad and dangerous work environment is tolerated;
5. rivalry and elbowing prevail;
6. human contacts are to a large extent replaced by communication through computers.

If the economic position of the whole country is strained and, at the same time, a high material standard of living is the overriding value, this scenario might become a reality. This would occur particularly when, in addition, technological development were regarded as a natural force which mankind cannot control. The degree of discomfort entailed in this scenario would depend to a certain extent on the length of the working day. If the working day is only, say, three hours, then it is much easier to put up with bad working conditions than if the working day is eight hours. The shorter the exposure to a bad work environment, the less severe the effects, one must assume. It is therefore to be expected that a substantial reduction in working hours might foster a trend in the direction of this scenario. This would be irrespective of the causes of shorter working hours, e.g. whether they were due to work-sharing or the result of the economy being so efficient that only short contributions are needed to maintain a high standard of living.

Scenario III shows a picture of the future that may seem both tempting and thrilling but also unrealistic. Many people might regard it as a mixture of nostalgia and social science fiction. But to some it is a conscious goal for social reformation. However, it raises the following questions:

1. How can one split up and decentralize the big companies?
2. Is it possible to scrap the big department stores and get the small shops back?

3. For what purposes could the big hospital buildings, some of which were built as late as the seventies, be used?

4. Would it be possible to get support for the goal of reducing the material standard of living?

5. Would it be possible for Sweden to pursue this line of development if other countries take an opposite course?

Of the three pictures of an imaginable future, the third is probably the most revolutionary compared with the present. Scenario I is an already established track. Scenario II may be seen as an unfortunate derailment, whereas Scenario III forms a big bend in the track that makes it change its course. It is true that there are already some small tendencies in this direction (delegation and decentralization as organizational principles), but these are only minor variations within the limits of the old track.

Section 3
Conflicts and Contradictions:
Some Typical Positions

edited by

MAURICE DE MONTMOLLIN

Introduction

MAURICE DE MONTMOLLIN

This Section deals with a number of perspectives in work psychology, drawing particularly on French authors. Chapters 10–13 are concerned with "real" problems in the world of work and organizations and the multi-disciplinary approaches which have been developed to deal with these problems. The later chapters discuss some of the ideological issues which need to be considered.

The editor of this Section is the author of Chapter 10. He is a relatively well-known, but not always appreciated work psychologist, who was for twenty five years a consultant, mainly in the field of ergonomics, and who is now a professor (University Paris-Nord and Ecole Polytechnique). Ergonomics ("cognitive ergonomics", which is a French speciality) has been his major professional interest, but he is also concerned with conditions of the work psychologists.

Chapter 11 is by Michèle Lacoste, who shows that work psychology is not practised exclusively by work psychologists. Coming from the exotic field of linguistics, with a stop-over in socio-linguistics, she is now working, as *Maître-assistant*, in the *Groupe Communication et Travail* at the University of Paris-Nord, where she is contributing, along with ergonomists and sociologists, to the analysis of different work situations. Her unpublished thesis is an extremely stimulating contribution to the analysis and interpretation of the interactions between physicians (who are also workers!) and their patients. Due to the unusual features of her approach, M. Lacoste was invited to write a chapter devoted mainly to the methodological aspects of her work.

Jacques Naymark is a young French psychologist, who recently spent three years in the Ivory Coast as a special adviser on the conception and implementation of a new government centre for the training of technical instructors. His practical experience led him to change from an enthusiastic, didactic, technocratic expert, to a more doubting and, probably, more effective trainer. The main reasons for this transformation are set out in his contribution. They underline that the psychologist also needs to take into account economic and sociological factors if his work is not to become sterile.

Frank Heller is director of the Centre for Decision Making Studies, Tavistock Institute of Human Relations. He has an international reputation as a researcher and a consultant, who has published widely. Chapter 13 is an updated version of his chairman's address to the Occupational Psychology Section of the British Psychological Society in 1973. In it he reflects on four problem areas which he feels may threaten the application of work psychology in the complexities of modern work organizations. Heller's contribution also provides a bridge between the theme of the earlier and later parts of this section, because he recognizes the ideological issues confronting work psychologists.

The question of *ideological backgrounds* is the theme of Chapters 14–16. The editor contributes a chapter on "Taylorism Today and its Contradictions" (Chapter 14). Taylorism, as a general ideology, is now loudly condemned, being officially replaced by a whole variety of humanistic concepts. However, it is argued that, in practice, Taylorism *is* the root ideology of the modern work psychologist, which leads to many contradictions. In Chapter 15, Enzo Spaltro, who has already been introduced in the previous Section of this book, describes ideological conflicts from the perspective of an Italian work psychologist. Italy is probably now the best European "laboratory" for the study of such conflicts and Spaltro's contribution is an excerpt from a much longer paper on the subject. Finally, in Chapter 16, Milton Hakel, who is a professor in I/O psychology at the Ohio State University, gives his impression of the challenges of diversity in the European scene, on the basis of his own experience. He has not only travelled widely in Europe, but has also worked closely with the editors and other contributors to this book. In 1978 he spent some months in Italy on a Fulbright fellowship.

10 Real Problems and Multidisciplinary Approaches

MAURICE DE MONTMOLLIN

The work psychologist is supposed to study, and even solve, "real" problems in the world of work and organizations. What does "real" mean in this context? To answer this question fully would lead to a metaphysical debate. For our purposes "real" characterizes problems which are not chosen or even created by the psychologist himself as is customary and legitimate, e.g. in the field of experimental psychology. The "real" problems confronting the work psychologist are presented by people who are not psychologists. Therefore, whereas the experimental psychologist defines his own concepts and variables, e.g. concerning the perception of space, the work psychologist is confronted with alien concepts, such as absenteeism or accident prevention, and has to subordinate his methods — that is the choice of his variables — to the complex "reality" of the situation in which he is operating.

Although this distinction is not always so sharp, it allows us to characterize roughly the evolution of work psychology. At the beginning, it was a variety of "applied" psychology, that is the application of a single, academic discipline to a specific domain of social life. The main example is selection, in which differential psychology is applied to the problem of hiring people. Similar features can be seen in the early development of ergonomics or human engineering. For example, the numerous studies of visual displays probably derived from the fact that experimental psychologists had developed methods for the study of visual perception, rather than from the actual needs of the military and industrial sponsors of such research. Experimental psychologists did not ask their clients: "What are your problems?" Instead they asked: "Have you any problems concerning perception?" Fortunately they had some but these were not necessarily the most important ones. In these fortuitous circumstances it was possible to find a lot of money for psychological research, whether it was relevant or not.

In some instances scientists created their methodological tools *before* applying them to the corresponding problems in organizations. After the application of differential psychology in hiring people, we have seen, for instance, the application of programmed learning in training them and the application of group dynamics to make them work happily together. But, at present, things are changing for the unfortunate work psychologist. It is less and less possible for him to select his problems in accordance with his methodological possibilities and interests. Psychological "gadgets" are now difficult to sell and there is no longer a market for some earlier approaches. The work psychologist can remain an expert in the mathematical analysis of tests, or a specialist in questionnaire building, or an ergonomist exclusively concerned with vigilance tasks. But, when the organization has immediate and difficult problems, e.g. of conflicts between engineers and salesmen, it is these which managers want to solve and not those within the psychologist's narrow areas of expertise. As noted in the early chapters of this book, the domain is constantly changing and clients are now posing questions to which there are no ready answers.

We thus have a situation in which the work psychologist is less and less allowed to remain the specialist of one discipline as he is confronted increasingly with problems characterized by diverse and mixed variables. As a "generalist", he must at least try to solve these problems, but paradoxically, as a scientist he has to use a multitude of different disciplines nevertheless.

Even in the field of psychology itself, there are several approaches: examples are differential psychology and psychometrics for selection and assessment; experimental psychology and sometimes psychophysiology for many ergonomics problems; clinical psychology for interviewing and counselling people. In addition, social psychologists are engaged in studying how people in organizations communicate with one another and form groups. And from child psychology have emerged some Piagetian approaches which have been applied to the cognitive aspects of working (Vermersch, 1978).

In the world of work, however, psychologists have to be familiar with and take account of a number of non-psychological disciplines. For example, every time a training programme is established it is likely to draw on elements of pedagogy. Likewise, to account for wages, salaries, job evaluation, it is necessary to be aware of economic principles and methods of analysis and knowledge of the law is essential when dealing with conflicts, strikes, negotiations, and personnel policy. Other relevant disciplines are: physiology and medicine for ergonomics and the design of man–machine systems; engineering in any factory; linguistics and semiology for man–man and man–machine communications. And, of course, in dealing with organizations of any kind, sociological theory and analysis are complementary to those of psychology.

If one takes this list of disciplines as essential knowledge for the practitioner, it would seem that the task of work psychologists has become impossible. There are not many supermen in the profession capable of blending the many different approaches into some synthetic applied science as the general practitioner is supposed to do. Nevertheless, in spite of this distressing situation, work psychologists continue to operate and to "ply their trade". The following suggestions arise from their experience.

1. First of all, there is some indication that organizations which offer the greatest opportunity for both study *and* action are the structured *medium sized* organizations: factories, offices, hospitals, schools, and so on. Work psychology cannot be reduced to the psychology of individual people, as it was (and still is) when concerned with selection procedures, which are sterile if not connected with the hiring organizational milieu. Nor can it be reduced to the workplace, as in the case of the engineer designing man–machine relationships, unless complemented by such considerations as the training of operators and shop-floor relationships. Work psychology, on the other hand, cannot be extended to general work sociology, which conducts analysis at the macro level where one cannot control the social variables. If he is to be an agent of change, it is imperative that the new work psychologist

should control some social variables. Thus, medium-sized structures, which have not been the subject of sufficient study by work psychologists so far (in Europe at least), could provide more opportunities to improve the present state of the art and lessen the contradictions between disciplinary orthodoxy and relevance. To alter the design of a display allows the work psychologist to be extremely scientific, but that happens very rarely. To change the morale of a whole company is extremely important, but practically impossible. To cut down the accident rate in a workshop, or lessen absenteeism in an office, could be technically feasible as well as leading to increased efficiency.

2. Secondly, perhaps the discipline which must be strongly promoted by the new work "psychology" is sociology. Sociology has been underestimated by psychologists, especially in Europe (in the United States, organizational psychology consists of a part of what we call here "sociology of work"). The psychological tradition considers people as individuals; nevertheless work is never realized individually but in organizations, with their traditions, rules, conflicts, ideologies. Academically social psychology was supposed to complement the individualistic approach, but has limited its approach mainly to small groups; and organizations are not small groups. Work sociology and organizational sociology can thus provide us with a lot of relevant material, concerning, for instance, industrial relations, which cannot be reduced to face-to-face bargaining but have to take into account the power structure of different social groups. Similarly, it emphasizes that the division of work cannot be considered by the psychologist as a purely technical or economical matter but must be seen also as a managerial weapon. The same applies to motivation, a traditional topic of work psychology, which cannot be modelled without reference to sociological data concerning absenteeism and turnover, in relation to such phenomena as unemployment, wages, size of enterprise.[1] One of the main difficulties which work psychologists experience in trying to collaborate with sociologists is that the latter are generally not interested in interventions. They like to analyse and

---

[1] An American image of the complementarity of the two approaches (traditional work psychology and work sociology) is given by the handbooks edited by Dunnette (1976) and Dubin (1976). In my opinion, the chapters concerning motivation, for instance, are more relevant in Dubin's handbook (the more sociological one), even from a "psychological" perspective.

describe things, but not to modify them, at least directly. And this attitude is not without consequence on their methods of analysis themselves, which often are too macroscopic to be useful. There is a need for researches concerning "mesoscopic" analysis.

3. Third, some even more specific recommendations can be advanced concerning diagnosis:

i. Work psychologists should be problem centred, not discipline centred. They should not only accept but emphasize the fact that they can neither choose nor construct their research problems. In the wider environment, psychology is of little interest in itself. The Chapter by Naymark is a good example of what happens when problems are approached exclusively from a disciplinary perspective. To achieve results, the practitioner had to broaden his outlook to include social and economic factors rather than concentrating on educational technology. In other words, people are not just the "subjects" of psychological experiments, the results of which will be judged by fellow academics: they inhabit a world with its own rules and standards of evaluation.

ii. There is a need to develop something that is more of an art than a science, that is the methodological know-how concerning work analysis. "Work analysis" is used here in its European sense, identification and measurement of the different variables determining the task to be done, the activity of the worker accomplishing this task, and the physical and organizational milieu surrounding the workplace. This is essential for a problem-centred approach. One cannot know what the problems really are without analysing what the situation really is, using as few presuppositions as possible. Such analysis includes the interrelations between the worker and his "machine", co-workers, managers, and the total organization. The literature in this field is quite limited and frequently trivial.[1] In general, work analysis tends to be reduced to taxonomical classification, which is useless for modifying or teaching the work itself. Verbal and general descriptions of aptitudes and skills supposed to be required in performing the task are used in place of circumstantial

---

[1] In this field the European work psychologists can be proud, especially the French and the Belgian ones. Work analysis is further developed here than it is even in the United States (see, for instance, Ombredane and Faverge, 1955; Montmollin, 1974; Leplat and Cuny, 1977).

accounts of physical and mental activities. Diagnosis and work analysis have in the past been taken as not being problematic, but as routine when embarking on research or case studies. However, this "preliminary" stage should be the central one. If you can identify correctly the different variables, their level, their nature, their interconnections, then you have almost hit the target, that is identified the nature of the problem. But, if you "botch" this diagnostic analysis stage, you are inclined to select only the issues which fit in with your own disciplinary perspectives. The more common examples are still with selection. There is a great danger that some psychologists will reduce organizational problems to the sole issue of hiring or promoting people able to fit the job, and thus ignore the wider organizational problems.

Of course, methods of diagnosis and analysis are not absolutely "discipline-free". For example, in the following pages there is an excellent account by Michèle Lacoste of the use of some new linguistic tools to analyse verbal interaction in a workshop. But the "art" of analysis requires the progressive integration of all the possibilities provided by different disciplines (see Ombredane and Faverge, 1955). Such integration is only at its beginning and is an essential if never-ending process. Fortunately, it is easier to integrate the methods of analysis provided by the different disciplines than it is to integrate the disciplines themselves.

In the past the emphasis in psychology was on methods of data analysis and this is still true to some extent. Now, and in the future, the emphasis should be on methods of data collection. The central problem is not how to use efficient methods for the interpretation of data, such as factor analysis or analysis of variance, but how to develop relevant methods (and the models underlying these methods) for the acquisition of data, such as better interviews, improved real life observations, recordings of social interactions and so on.

4. Finally, to be more "problem centred" than "discipline centred" does not mean that we have to be "discipline ignorant". To study and modify work is mainly an art, but this art cannot survive if it is not supported by the various scientific disciplines. Thus, the contradictions between the theoretical necessity and the practical impossibility of setting up a well-defined multidisciplinary approach still remain. Consequently, work psychology cannot hope to become a coherent and

harmonious whole for a long time. We have to endure a situation in which we cannot be pure scientists like the experimental psychologists, nor yet be effective practitioners like the physicians. We have to learn to live with this contradiction, that is, we should not deny it nor minimize it.[1] Herein lies the root of many of the problems experienced by work psychologists.

References

DE MONTMOLLIN, M. (1974). *L'Analyse du Travail.* A. Colin, Paris.

DUBIN, R. (ed.) (1976). *Handbook of Work, Organization and Society.* Rand McNally, Chicago.

DUNNETTE, M. D. (ed.) (1976). *Handbook of Industrial and Organizational Psychology.* Rand McNally, Chicago.

LEPLAT, J. AND CUNY, X. (1977). *Introduction à la Psychologie du Travail.* P.U.F., Paris.

OMBREDANE, A. AND FAVERGE, J. M. (1955). *L'Analyse du Travail.* P.U.F., Paris.

VERMERSCH, P. (1978). Une problématique théorique en psychologie du travail. Essais d'application des théories de J. Piaget à l'analyse du fonctionnement cognitif de l'adulte. *Le Travail Humain*, 41, 265–280.

---

[1] This problem is now extensively discussed in the *Société d'Ergonomie de Langue Française* (French-speaking Society of Ergonomics).

11 Language and Communication for Work Analysis

MICHÈLE LACOSTE

A. Language and interaction in the study of social communication

Internal necessities in their respective studies have caused certain schools of thought in both linguistics and sociology to move closer together. Linguistics, by directing its attention to the use of language, has had to find a place for social and situational factors; sociology, facing up to the fact that it is constantly referring to language events (interviews, questionnaires) has been considering the relevance of analytic procedures developed by linguists. This convergence has opened up a range of wide and varied perspectives, which we shall set out here in broad outline.

First of all, there has been a genuine discovery of spoken language in everyday life. In spite of their declarations of principle, linguists have previously given this scant attention. A change occurred when sociolinguistics adopted a new theoretical instrument (insisting on the socialized character of language) and the tape-recorder provided an appropriate technical breakthrough. For here we have the necessary conditions whereby the recording of and listening to speech gives access to the texture of spoken language. This gives a plethora of facts which one cannot grasp in their entirety without these two instruments. Take, for example, the paralinguistic phenomena — intonation, pauses, speed of utterance — as well as the structure of oral discourse, which is different from the written and whose complex nature is only just beginning to be appreciated. Whereas written language presupposes that one masters more complex and more elaborate thinking (which explains the difficulty children have in acquiring it), spoken language is closer to the way we think in everyday life, when we come to grips with the practical world. If we accept this hypothesis, a new field of research opens up before us, the principle being to study oral discourse in daily life and, through discourse, to investigate the way in which people build up their relationships with their environment and with society. The methods and tools of analysis needed for this will be outlined in the course of this chapter.

The spoken word is the medium of verbal intercourse. Its normal use supposes two or more participants who speak, listen, take turns at talking, interrupting or not, all according to tacit but nonetheless binding rules. "Conversation analysis" has systematically explored the way in which language functions here, how speech partners take turns, insisting on incidents such as interruptions, excuses, silences and so on. These reveal the relationships between the speakers, their respective power, their understandings or their confrontations, including subtle power struggles, that cannot be inferred from formal definition of status and role. The proposition for a "grammar of conversations" with its precise rules, made by Sacks *et al.* (1974), marks a break with the usual quantitative accounts (based on the number of utterances by speaker, length of utterance, etc.) which while not being completely negligible, provide information which is superficial and of little meaning on its own. Thus the number of utterances a speaker makes does not necessarily reflect his real power; it is merely an indicator to be placed in the context of a fuller appreciation, a remark which would sound obvious and superfluous were it not for the large number of works which still make use of these rather mechanistic parameters.

Ethnomethodologists began by using the traditional systems of psychosociology such as that of Bales (1950). They came to the conclusion that this sort of categorization, based on a previous perfunctory classification (giving an opinion versus "a fact" versus "an orientation", etc.) made it necessary to start off by fixing the interpretation of discourse from the outset, instead of sticking closely to the details. This explains their subsequent search for a different, more rigorous systematization based on the analysis of recorded spoken data.

Speech is, after all, only one of the resources at the disposal of actors in what Goffman calls the stage setting of daily life, and where the idea of communication comes to the aid of the notion of discourse. In any environment and in any normal face-to-face activity, people act and mark out their reciprocal relationships through their physical behaviour (gestures, rhythms, postures, eye movements) and their way of occupying space. These types of behaviour are all the more meaningful as they often go unnoticed and are not submitted to official codification, and they are used in complex strategies. Goffman (1961, 1963) gives many examples of these types of behaviour in a work environment (hospitals, workshops, factories, schools) and it is no accident that he is at the same time the author of one of the most penetrating conversation analyses (1975). This is where there is a genuine convergence in perspective. The general framework has been made productive through confrontation with definite social practices and with fields of work that bring together many different social and technical factors.

B. Sociolinguistic analyses from the viewpoint of work

Although these analyses of conversation and the nature of verbal interaction have been adopted effectively in different spheres (school, delinquency, street culture) the idea of using them in research on the problems of work is only just beginning to have an impact. Developments such as interactionist sociology and strategic analysis have made their appearance in this field and thereby drawn attention to instances of communication, but the collecting and treating of these data lags behind the partial changes in the models of analysis. Thus we shall insist here on the importance of collecting varied verbal data and the use of depth analysis procedures.

An initial study (Lacoste, 1976) in a hospital environment enabled us to observe and record medical consultations and analyse the dynamics of intercourse between patient and doctor. In the medical field evaluating and measuring is not the easiest of tasks, and quite possibly the nature of medical work itself does not lend itself to simple definition. But keeping in mind how things get done aided the linguistic observation and the linguistic observation, in its turn, gave new arguments for an analysis of activities.

In this connection there was one question which stood out above all others, namely, which cases represented merely the socially defined ritual with the outward form of a consultation (doctor's questions and patient's answers, examination, prescription), but without anything really happening? In which cases was a diagnosis really made, followed by medical advice, understood and accepted by the patient? Specifically, is it possible to distinguish between a real consultation and a mere ritual? It is obvious that an exhaustive answer to this query cannot be given here, but we have noted and systematically studied certain meaningful indicators in the spoken intercourse: (1) linguistic indicators (for example, the way of following on in the series of questions and answers between doctor and patient, the differential treatment of certain themes in the course of the conversation the way they repeat or take up the other's speech, the internal contradictions in the discourse etc.); (2) communication factors (smiles, sighs, silences, changes in posture and position, the relationship between speech and certain physical acts on the part of the doctor). These patterns make it possible to characterize the types of consultation, according to the interaction strategies of the doctors or patients, leading to an analysis in terms of the success or failure of activities necessitating communication between doctor and patient.

Although this research concentrated on analysing precise and limited questions, the contribution of sociolinguistics and allied disciplines to the study of work can be viewed in a more general perspective. The widening of the framework of analysis and its adaptation to more symbolic and less directly productive activities than those of manual workers or even office staff is exemplified by research now underway on the subject of social workers, aimed at evaluating their practices. The transformation of the models of interpretation required to deal with the activities of these professional groups should have positive repercussions on the understanding of work in general. In the field of industry, current research makes it possible to sketch out certain guidelines. All these studies have been made in small-scale units (lines, workshops) whose members work in close interaction. The material gathered allows a qualitative depth analysis of which one example is presented here, stressing the methodology of observation and processing.

C. A study in industry: the case of a packaging workshop

This research took place in a highly automated soap packaging workshop where we had been approached by the management, who had in mind a job enrichment project. The workers, all women, were trained on the job of feeding and supervising the machines, which the management considered monotonous but not really tiring. This was the reason for the job enrichment project. It was received negatively by the women, who saw in it the threat of an increase in work. An article published by the team responsible for this research (Craipeau, de Montmollin, Potier, 1978) came to the conclusion that job restructuring was needed rather than job enrichment. In the course of the observation, in which the author participated actively, and the following analysis, we used procedures derived from socio-linguistics and conversation analysis. The data recorded for this analysis were mainly of two kinds: (1) shop floor meetings, categorized as "natural conversations", i.e. socially determined but not prompted by the research and (2) interviews.

We shall devote the remainder of the chapter to examining these two sets of data:

1. THE SHOPFLOOR MEETING

In a business or workshop, "natural conversations" may take various forms such as meetings, fact-to-face communication between mobile workers (executives, foremen, certain workers) or between these and non-mobile workers, conversations between the workers during breaks or, during working hours, hand waving or some short sentences shouted above the general noise. These forms of communication may be necessitated by work roles or be unconnected with them, even going as far as secret exchanges. These sorts of verbal behaviour, which form the basis of day-to-day relationships, have often been neglected, or relatively little explored. Our orientation brings them to the foreground.

We analysed particularly the recordings of meetings organized by the management to inform workers about problems of safety and the functioning of the workshop (Bachmann and Simonin, 1978). These meetings were recorded by two trainee students, with the agreement of those taking part. The example we shall take is of a preparatory meeting in which the personnel manager and the technical manager were getting together with the foremen to decide how the foremen would approach the workers. The personnel manager wanted to seize the opportunity of the shopfloor meetings to clear up the problem of output. In this firm, output has no effect on pay, monthly salaries having been introduced at the same time as mechanization. However, psychological pressure is brought to bear in that the foremen post up each woman's output every hour, and there is a running state of confusion between machine output, standard output and worker output, with the result that the women tend to underestimate their own output, which fosters in them a constant anxiety to work faster and faster.

What actually happened in the preparatory meeting? The first feeling of the student who recorded it was that it was a meeting devoid of any interest and that nothing happened. Indeed, no decision was taken explicitly and a good deal of breath was expended for apparently little outcome. However, on closer scrutiny, it may be seen that something had indeed taken place. The way the meeting evolved reflects the confrontation of two concepts of management in the firm, largely linked with the difference of functions, as there was opposition between the personnel manager, who wanted to tell the women the "whole truth" about output, and the technical manager, who wanted to maintain the status quo. The analysis of the recordings shows the shifting balance of power, partly arbitrated by the foremen, and the inter-action strategies of the participants. The failure to take a decision in fact takes on the sense of failure of the personnel manager's initiative.

In essence, four main phases could be discerned in the meeting. First, the personnel manager appeared to be successful in proposing to use the meeting to speak to the workers about output, as shown by the following brief extract:[1]

PERSONNEL MANAGER: So you see we can kill two birds with one stone, we can train them by explaining what output is, efficiency, worker output, machine output, standard output — we clarify the idea of output to put it all under one heading.

FOREMEN: Yes.

TECHNICAL MANAGER: On that very point, on output, I've got something all ready from when I took over packaging which can be used.

PERSONNEL MANAGER: Right. He'll give the lecture then.

[1] A non-technical transcription so as not to present inessential complications.

The personnel manager thinks he has won — he tries to close the debate ("Right") by snidely having the technical manager ("give the lecture") explain output to the workers.

The second phase was marked by the technical manager's first refusal:

TECHNICAL MANAGER: No I won't give any lecture.

leading to, third, a phase of digression into technicalities, showing a succession of fine movements with shifting balance of power. The fourth phase consisted of the final refusal by the technical manager, this time seconded by several foremen, which ended the meeting.

TECHNICAL MANAGER: No, we must keep machine time. Right, I think the first
        meeting . . .
PERSONNEL MANAGER: I think we'll have to come round to it one day — we'll just
        have to get round to this business.

The technical manager wins the day and finally closes the discussion ("Right"), so the problem of output will not be broached at the first meeting with the workers. The personnel manager may well finish on a threatening note ("We'll have to get round" to speaking about it), but he must give in for the moment (the sign of giving up is the use of the future — here *will* — instead of the present).

These data, analysed in detail and compared with other data, especially from later meetings with foremen and workers, opened the way for observation of the constitution of a social process, leading to a comprehensive study of work. Checking the contradictions of the situation in very great detail makes it possible to evaluate the conditions and the chances of success of the work organization project which first prompted the study.

On what procedure is the analysis based? We have already mentioned recording, guaranteeing the objective nature of the data. A transcription is then needed, where the details of the verbal exchange are noted (marked stress, pauses, overlapping speech, interruptions, etc.) so as to reproduce as faithfully as possible each speaker's share in the intercourse. This stage, of necessity quite technical, "freezes" speech, a necessary step to noting many significant details which go unnoticed even after repeated hearings.

The analysis presupposes an acquaintance with the situation, as is the case when the observer actually takes part in it. What is original about this method is the use of this ethnographic approach in conjunction with the analysis of language data as observable indicators of the interaction. In order to study the participants' strategies during the meeting, Bachmann and Simonin chose to concentrate on conversation indicators: pauses, overlapping and especially speech triggers (that is, the words or phrases beginning a speech). From this they obtained form patterns which varied in the course of the interaction, reflecting the shifts in the balance of power between the participants. This search for new indicators, going beyond the more strictly linguistic marks, should be extended in the future so as to include the relations of space, gesture and vision which go with social communication.

2.   INTERVIEWS WITH THE WOMEN

The "natural" conversations picked up in the course of observation were complemented by interviews. Can the interview, that familiar tool in the hands of the psychologist and the sociologist, be used equally well in the field of communication as described here? Can communication studies contribute to a new use and interpretation of the interview? Our answer to these questions is affirmative, provided certain conditions are met as to how the interview is carried out and how it is analysed.

The first condition is that the context of the interview must be made explicit. This implies not only indicating the pertinent macro-social factors but, more especially, an account of the physical conditions such as who prompted the interview, where did it take place, was the interviewer imposed by the organization, what were his strategies of presentation. Setting out this extralinguistic data systematically enables one to refer back and forth from language factors to situational factors, as the model is built up. The complementary nature of the two sorts of factors makes them inseparable. In other words, without the situation, there is no possible analysis of the discourse, except for tautological rephrasings or purely formal restructuring *in vacuo*; without language, there is nothing for the interpretation to fall back on. It is also a matter of common sense that the interview situation should not be too "formal" or there is the danger that it may become meaningless. Sociolinguistics is to be credited with attempting to determine the degree of formality, as defined by Labov (1972), in terms of the speaker's attention to the language he uses. This question is of course far too complex to be effectively measured by any unidimensional scale.

Finally, the interview is not to be considered as an atemporal event in the subject's experience, but as the product of a situation. The contents are not treated as unique, isolated data, but are placed in a set of verbal productions with which they are constantly compared. Thus, when the same theme — say an industrial accident — crops up several times (in interviews, in conversation between workers or at a meeting) a comparative analysis makes it possible to see the interpretation of one and the same event by the different social actors and to take account of the influence of the speech situation. Observing non-verbal, practical and other communication behaviour also makes an invaluable contribution to the analysis.

It was with this outlook and bearing these conditions in mind that the students acting as participant observers had conversations with the women working in the workshop (individually or in pairs). The opening gambit was ostensibly work to be done on a brochure on security, but the content was largely non-directive, touching on all aspects of life on the shopfloor, output, work on the machines, and so on.

How was the material treated? We shall simply give a far from exhaustive list of the main systems used in interpretation, without going into how they are linked together. It is important to bring all indicators into play systematically for, in the accounts which the women made of their work, the overt and immediate content is less significant than the fine discursive patterns, which generally escape the subject's attention.

At the beginning of the interview, the first words which the interviewee uses to answer the initial question are often very rich in significance and warrant a thorough study. For example, one of the women launched into her opinion on safety in these terms: "Not everyone is of the same opinion, but I think that the safety here (name of the firm) is good." This first statement contains a summary of the two main characteristics of this conversation: (1) an argumentative plan of the type "accusation/defence"; (2) a strategy of "prudence" with regard to the interviewer.

This remark leads us to the logico-rhetorical rules inherent in the nature of the "speech act" or "speech event", which are concepts defined by the pragmatics and ethnography of communication (see Hymes, 1972); the study of these rules can go far to account for the "natural logic" of the argument (Grize, 1974).

Let us return briefly to the aforementioned statement in the light of these lines of research. The statement may be divided into two substatements, noted here as S1 and S2:

S1: *I think that the safety here is good.*
   S1 = Evaluation (I think) + Sentence (the safety here is good).
S2: *Not everyone is of the same opinion.*
   S2 has two different interpretations, which may be formulated as follows:
   S2' = Not everyone agrees among themselves.
   S2" = Not everyone agrees with me.

Note that S1 (the "central" statement, which gives the information proper) is preceded by S2. This shows that the woman's discourse is built as a preconstructed discursive, based on previous discussions about safety in the firm, but also on what the woman thinks the interviewer expects. Note too that each of the two substatements S1 and S2 is ambiguous in the sense of allowing a double interpretation, indicating a general strategy of prudence to which the rest of the interview amply testifies. We have given the two possible meanings of S2. In the case of S1, the French expression *je trouve* (here: I think) has two usages: it may reinforce the statement by personalizing it or, on the contrary, it may lessen its impact by disclaiming universal acceptance of this option.

Other categories of analysis include the use of personal pronouns, verb tense, mood, spatial and temporal referents relating to the "statement" and the types of verbs or adjective relating to the "presupposition"; "moves", in Goffman's sense, denoting progress in the discourse; and changes of topic indicated by transitional constructions marking the change from one theme to another. Likewise, paralinguistic indicators such as laughter, smiles, intonation, speed of utterance, stress, pauses, need to be brought into focus with other significant factors. Although these elements have often been studied in the laboratory, they have seldom been examined in the context of daily conversation.

Accounting for these types of indicator allows one to treat discourse in many lights, looking for the substantive traces of deeper meaning.

From the study of language data hypotheses can be made about the processes underlying interaction, how people relate to different aspects of work and their attitude towards possible changes. In this study, the recorded interviews enabled several constructions of the micro-universe of the firm to be identified and characterized (e.g. workers' relationships to their machines, to technology, to the hierarchical organization, to other workers). After close and repeated analysis, certain interviews revealed unexpected contradictions. These reflected the women's contradictory and conflicting situation which led to their refusal of the job enrichment project. Thus, used in a comparative way, the interview turned out to be a valuable adjunct to the "natural" data.

The line of research outlined here points to ways in which an interdisciplinary approach can be developed as a necessary condition for progress in the analysis of work. Studies based on verbal interaction provide complementary and new kinds of data to those of the work psychologist and other specialists. They presuppose of course that ergonomics is not simply the study of the technical characteristics of a job, but includes the adaptation of man–machine systems as a complex feature of behaviour within the total setting of social interaction.

The potentialities of this approach are very great and studies to complement those set out here may be readily envisaged. A study is already under way on a very precise topic to grasp the understanding that unskilled women workers have of the jobs they are doing by analyzing their discursive logic in predetermining situations such as explaining to a new worker how a machine works, telling the observer why a technical fault occurred, and so on. Other studies could be defined more broadly, some of which call for a study of the upper levels of the hierarchy and a more comprehensive knowledge of the firm.

This paper has demonstrated that the problematics and methodology exist, with their own techniques. It is hoped that the field of investigation, still in its infancy, will grow and extend in the years ahead.

References

BACHMANN, CH. AND SIMONIN, J. (1978). Unpublished communication at the *Table Ronde sur les données sociolinguistique dans l'analyse du milieu de travail*, Paris.

BALES, R. F. (1950). A set of categories for the analysis of small group interaction. *American Sociological Review,* 15, 257–263.

CRAIPEAU, S., DE MONTMOLLIN, M. AND POTIER, S. (1978). Enrichissement des tâches ou restructuration des tâches? Le cas d'un atelier de conditionnement. *Le Travail Humain,* 41, 33–42.

GOFFMAN, E. (1961). *Encounters.* Bobbs-Merrill, Indianapolis.

GOFFMAN, E. (1963). *Behavior in Public Places.* The Free Press, New York.

GOFFMAN, E. (1975). Replies and responses. Working Paper n°46–47, Centro Internazionale di Semiotica e Linguistica, Urbino.

GRIZE, J. B. (ed.) (1974). Recherches sur le discours et l'argumentation. Special issue of *Revue Européenne des Sciences Sociales et Cahiers Vilfredo Pareto,* 12, No. 32. Editions Droz, Genève.

HYMES, D. (1972). The ethnography of speaking. In *Readings in the Sociology of Language* (Fishman, J., ed.). La Haye, Mouton, Paris.

LACOSTE, M. (1976). Analyse sociolinguistique de consultations médicales hospitalières. Unpublished Thesis, Université de Paris-Nord.

LABOV, W. (1972). *Sociolinguistics Patterns.* University of Pennsylvania Press, Philadelphia.

SACKS, H., SCHEGLOFF, E., JEFFERSON, G. (1974). A simplest systematics for the organization of turn-taking for conversation. *Language,* no. 50.

12 Observations on Vocational Training in the Ivory Coast

This chapter discusses the problems set by vocational training in an industrially developing country such as the Ivory Coast, based on the author's first-hand experience.

What are the characteristics of the psychologist's job whose role it is to implement this training in a socio-cultural context which is both different from and quite similar to his own? These similarities and differences arise from colonial history and the present demands of industrial rationalization.

Within a short paper, it is impossible to deal with all the intricate problems set by training in developing countries. Therefore, these questions will be discussed in the context of an experiment concerned with a new training system introduced by the Ministry of Technical Education and Vocational Training.

A. The training system

Great changes are occurring in the educational system of the Ivory Coast under the combined pressure of two factors, which are found in most developing countries:

1. a rapid economic expansion (7% per annum);
2. a population explosion (4% per annum): the current population

131

comprises 7000 000 inhabitants of whom 800 000 are students in elementary schools, 115 000 are in secondary schools, 10 000 in technical colleges and 10 000 in institutes of higher education.

Here, it is necessary to bear in mind that the present educational system, for obvious reasons, is based on that in France, where it has been criticized for some time. The transfer of that system to a different socio-cultural and economical environment serves to make it something of a caricature.

The recommendations of the 1976–80 Ivory Coast Development Plan are to be seen in this context. This plan requires the training system to "consider the national realities, the technological components of the modern economy and the real needs of development more seriously" as well as to set up "crash programmes to train the staff and technicians necessary for the rapid "ivorization" of jobs and decision-making centres" (5-year Plan 1976–80).

Implementation of this Plan rests on three complementary systems:

a. *Basic vocational training*. This is intended for youths coming from general education at various levels. It is a training programme to prepare them for a job and for working life. Therefore the curricula are worked out on the basis of job descriptions. This approach demands a specific pedagogy, now in the process of being tested in a pilot vocational Lycée.

b. *Further vocational training*. This aims at improving the training of people already in office and to make their promotion easier.

c. *The training of trainers*. This is the most important instrument in the setting of the two previous systems. It has two imperatives:

    1. to train the trainers for the opening of vocational Lycées;

    2. to train trainers who are better adapted to pedagogical patterns and practices.

These trainers are intended to become the "initiators of change" in the educational system.

In this chapter two aspects are treated in particular:

    1. the use of a specific pedagogy linked to vocational training;

    2. the training of trainers.

B.   Pedagogy by instructional objectives

This kind of pedagogical approach, which is unusual in France, is derived mainly from the American works of Bloom (Krathwohl *et al.*, 1969, 1970), Gagné (1965), and Mager (1962), and introduced by De Landsheere (1976). It is a pedagogy which aims at setting "learning situations", and facilitating them through a focus on the learning process rather than the teaching process. In other words, the learner is at the centre of the pedagogical process.

This procedure has a double objective:

i. rationalizing the educational system;
ii. increasing the autonomy of the learner.

Thus, the aim is to define minimal threshold levels which can be reached by anybody and thus avoid having a training programme which can be completed only by the most able.

The first application of these concepts in the Ivory Coast is taking place in a tertiary vocational Lycée intended to train secretaries, accountants, and commercial agents.

The new training plans have been defined jointly by representatives of the Ministry of Technical Education and the employers and teachers concerned, according to the following procedure:

i. Identification of job descriptions for secretarial work and accountancy (job profiles).
ii. Job analysis.
iii. Definition of the general objectives of training.
iv. Transformation of the general objectives into specific units of observable behaviour.
v. Construction of the training programme in three modules:
1. a common core of basic subjects;
2. a specialization phase with a choice of options (secretarial work or accountancy);
3. a professionalization phase preparatory to the job.

In practice, after a year, this programme encountered much resistance from the various people concerned: decision makers, trainers, students. It turned out that the transformation of a system focused on the educational content to one focused on the learner is extremely difficult to achieve. Some of the professionals responsible for the change are so excited by the new "educational technologies" that they become the "sorcerer's apprentices" of the pedagogy. Thus, the favourite topic of many trainers of trainers is self-development, self-training, and self-documentation. Although this approach is potentially very fertile, at present it does not match any practical demand. For example, the students' autonomy, which is one of the main objectives, is discouraged when any demand for information is evaluated as showing incapacity to learn in an autonomous way.

At a minimum, it appears that the teachers who are summarily trained for the "instructional objectives pedagogy", are reluctant to participate. Prisoners of traditional patterns, they are disturbed by the many references in their training to various psychological theories, such as behaviourism (Skinner, Gagné), cognition (Piaget, Bruner), or mentalism (Bloom). These trainers, whether they are French technical assistants (many of whom are in technical education) or Ivory Coast nationals, have all been shaped by a tradition where the mastering of content prevailed, and, therefore, are not very interested in psycho-pedagogy and educational theories. For them, teachers are born, not made, and they think that "pedagogy is an art, it cannot be learnt!"

From the students' point of view, a purely vocational training is not attractive. Vocational Lycées prepare them for degrees which give no direct access to higher education. This measure is designed to prevent the overproduction of university graduates in subjects with no vocational openings. However, students perceive higher education as a route to progression up the status hierarchy.

There is clearly a gap between the objectives of the Ministry's decision-makers and the students' values and perceptions. As noted above, the Ministry's aim is to improve the balance between training and the production needs of the country's development. However, the students cling to more classical values, stemming from the colonial period, where to study meant to become "a big wheel" (minister, director, lawyer, civil servant). It is therefore apparent that there is a distortion, not to say a paradox, between the objectives of the training system and students' expectations based on the myth of social success through education.

It is too early to draw any definite conclusion from this experiment. Nevertheless, in the light of similar experiments in Algerian Technological Institutes, the main criticism to be made of such training is that it is tied to job recruitment in too narrow and utilitarian a manner. As a result, it may jeopardize the promotion of the "products" of the system.

It is obvious that industrial and economic considerations have determined the educational and, therefore, the pedagogical choices of the Development Plan, and not humanistic or cultural preoccupations. One may regret the absence of general culture in the training procedure, which is now considered to be too theoretical and responsible for the inadequacy of the previous pattern. Therefore, we can say that we are confronted with a basic contradiction.

C. The training of trainers

The need to train trainers capable of applying the pedagogical procedures seems obvious, but the recruitment of these trainers sets serious problems.

In the first place, industrial development puts heavy pressures on the local employment market. One consequence of a tight labour market (60 000 workers in the industrial sector in 1976) is that recruitment of competent trainers takes place against competition from private firms which, in certain cases, offer material conditions superior to those of the Administration. In 1978, the IPNETP (National Pedagogical Institute for Technical Education and Vocational Training) sought to recruit a number of trainers in accountancy, but only two candidates (for about 15 jobs) came forward! At comparable levels the salaries offered in the private sector were fifty per cent higher than those offered in public education. For vocational training instructors however, the situation was reversed with 120 candidates applying for four positions. These recruitment problems, although not unexpected, have only been taken into account to a limited extent. If a recruitment service, responsible for standardizing European or American psycho-technical tests, were to be created for the African population, it does not mean that the problem would be solved. The success of the recruitment programme is entirely dependent at present on financial considerations. Under these circumstances, psychologists who limit their horizons to the pedagogical aspects cannot be effective.

Therefore, in spite of the considerable sums invested in training, the proportion of national trainers remains low and technical education is still highly dependent on French technical assistants. At present, the number of national trainers of trainers is almost equal to the number of trainees!

These serious difficulties indicate the need to take account of the balance between economic factors and available human resources. This is one of the classical problems of developing countries which has not yet entered the psychologist's or the trainer's field of vision.

D.   Some conclusions

It is desirable that the psychologist who works in developing countries should reflect deeply and constantly on the whole cultural and socioeconomic environment in which his work takes place. If he does not do so he is liable to become confined in the "ivory tower" of a specialist with sophisticated but inapplicable methods; or, even more seriously, as an expert with a lot of power he may engage in projects which are irrelevant to the real needs and requirements of the country.

In the author's experience, training, as a development factor, seems invested with a power disproportionate to the practical answers it brings. A serious evaluation of the impact of training on the development of a country would certainly throw some light on the situation. From such a perspective, the main factor is the rate at which an agrarian society changes to an industrialized society, rather than the educational techniques in use. Some pedagogical institutes in the Ivory Coast look like real cathedrals in a desert, gathering the most elaborate equipment available in the field of technology applied to education. One cannot help but wonder about the wisdom of introducing expensive educational technologies out of their cultural and social context. It seems that the industrially developing countries are the last resort of those who wish to undertake educational experiments!

Finally, it can be said that, in spite of many economic and socio-cultural barriers, the developing countries do not avoid the standardization imposed by industrial rationalization (Wisner, 1976). Far from being an esoteric area of research, the study of the transfer of technological and educational processes from industrialized to developing countries will help us to understand some of the phenomena of hyper-developed countries. In particular, it will throw light on issues which are not readily isolated in more complex societies.

References

DE LANDSHEERE, G. (1976). *La Formation des Enseignants Demain.* Casterman, Paris.

DE LANDSHEERE, G. AND DE LANDSHEERE, V. (1976). *Définir les Objectifs de l'Education.* P.U.F., Paris.

GAGNÉ, R. (1965). *The Conditions of Learning.* Holt, Rinehart and Winston, New York.

GOBLE, N. AND PORTER, F. (1977). *L'Evolution du Rôle du Maître.* UNESCO, Paris.

KRATHWOHL, D. R., BLOOM, B. S. AND MASIA, B. B. (1969 and 1970). *Taxonomie des Objectifs Pédagogiques.* Trad. Française, 2 vol. Education Nouvelle, Montréal.

MAGER, R. F. (1962). *Preparing Instructional Objectives.* Fearon, Palo-Alto.

MCLAUGHLIN, S. AND MOULTON, J. (1976). *L'Evaluation des Méthodes de Formation par Performance. Manuel à l'Usage des Formateurs de Maîtres.* UNESCO, Paris.

PLAN QUINQUENNAL 1976-1980. Ministère du Plan, République de Côte d'Ivoire.

WISNER, A. (1976). Existe-t-il une ergonomie propre aux pays en voie de développement? In *Pratique de l'Ergonomie et Pays en Développement Industriel.* Rapport No 52, CNAM, Paris.

13 Problem Areas in the Psychology of Work

FRANK A. HELLER

The view put forward in this chapter is quite simple. Over the last fifty years we have accumulated a proud and valuable tradition for scientific as well as practical work in our area of psychology. Some part of this tradition however is no longer useful and may even hold us up. Four potentially serious stumbling blocks should receive our attention.

A. Academic boundary disputes

To begin with there are academic boundary disputes. What are the limits of our territory and where are the rich areas in it?

A review of recent conferences in different parts of the world and the literature relevant to a modern conception of the personnel function (Heller and Clark, 1976) would include at least the following:

devising and monitoring organizational change
managerial leadership
the quality of organizational life
participation, co-determination and self-management
studies of motivation at various organizational levels
multinational or cross-cultural comparisons in various areas of our work

studies in decision making
mid career development problems
the effect of the organizational environment on people
innovation and creativity
psychological studies of strikes and conflict
the utilization of existing skills
manpower planning and assessment at the level of the firm
job alienation and the effect of unemployment
study of values and ethical considerations in organizational life
the effect of automation
design of organizations and policies
the organization and structure of small work groups
job design
the effect of uncertainty, pressure and control
the effect of competition, cooperation, conformity and cohesiveness
   of work groups
resistance to change
the study of organizational goals

This list suggests the possibility of extending our range of interest for the psychology of work. This has practical as well as theoretical implications, for instance, for curricula construction in university courses.

It can be argued that psychologists who deal with problems arising out of the activity of work in modern organizations have in fact tackled a wide variety of topics, though it is true to say that many of the less traditional fields were pioneered in the United States and that practitioners in some of them would not describe themselves as psychologists. If we start an analysis, possibly even an evaluation, of our present and future spheres of activities, the question to be asked is something like this: Given that we have been successful in handling many of the traditional subject areas in our field of psychology and that we should clearly continue with most of them in the future, what additional problem areas should or could be identified for more concentrated attention?

In making our choice we should pay attention to three factors:

a. our own interests and professional skills;
b. the changing nature of occupations and organizations in the present and future decades; and

c. the requirements of client groups, including in particular the relatively neglected area of industrial relations and topics identified as important by trade unions.

With regard to the first factor, our skills, particularly our methodological skills, are well advanced and can make a very useful contribution to a wide variety of areas of scientific inquiry. The advantage psychologists have over some other social sciences is precisely in our range of methodology and in our rigorous approach to problems.

The second and third factors require special attention. Have we taken sufficient care to anticipate the future? Do we agree or disagree with Drucker's *Age of Discontinuity* (1968), Alvin Toffler's *Future Shock* (1970), Herman Kahn's *The Year 2000* (Kahn and Wiener, 1967), Daniel Bell's *The Coming of Post-Industrial Society* (1976), Fred Hirsch's *Social Limits to Growth* (1977), Emery and Trist's *Towards a Social Ecology* (1973), Don Mankin's *Towards a Post-Industrial Psychology* (1978) and Kerr and Rosow's *Work in America: The Decade Ahead*?

Many will argue that there is a lot of loose thinking in these futuristic exercises, but are they completely wrong? Each of these authors makes assumptions which, if correcct, would vitally affect the nature of man's work, that is to say, our special field of expertise. Is there a danger that we are allowing events to overtake us? Are we confident that by the year 2000 our standard fields of work and our current research preferences will enable occupational psychologists to tackle the important problems — even if only one in a hundred of the crystal-gazing anticipations come off? Young people of say 25 who qualify today in our field of psychology will only be 44 years old in the year 2000. Will they have to retire prematurely because their skills will not match the problems of that period which is only just ahead of us?

B. Scientism

Secondly, there is the problem which can be termed "Holier than thou scientism".

Scientism provides two traps for social scientists; firstly there is the temptation to imitate the physical sciences when this is not appropriate.

Because of the high prestige of the physical sciences and their long successful development this trend is understandable, although it can be argued that by giving in to the temptation, we are delaying our own process of maturation and are heaping on to ourselves the kind of criticism which comes from using a tennis racket in a game of ping pong. The tool may be powerful but it is neither relevant nor effective for the purpose.

The second trap is the consequence of trying to copy the methods of the physical sciences but not really understanding what they are. This is the view of Popper who believes that all scientific endeavour including sociology, psychology, economics and physics uses the hypothetic deductive method and achieves progress by building patiently bit by bit through the analysis of practical technological investigations of practical technological problems (Popper, 1957, pp. 58–60). More recently a similar point was made by Carl Rogers (1973). Rogers also quoted the physicist Robert Oppenheimer who warned the American Psychological Association in 1956 that the worst thing psychology might do would be "to model itself after a physics which is not there any more, which has been outdated" (Oppenheimer, 1956, p. 134).

By contrast with Popper's approach social scientists are often busy with one or more of the following activities, which they fondly believe to be the prestige activities of "science":

1. producing grand abstract theories;
2. grovelling in volumes of objective data and "sorting them out" into conclusions;
3. stating broad universalistic generalizations; and
4. assuming or deducing causal relations between variables based on laws of determinism.

The third of these imagined activities of science is discussed below and the fourth is discussed in the next section.

The universalistic generalization takes the form of a statement that a certain variable, high intelligence for instance, leads to certain consequences, let us say success in a given job category. I know this problem best in research on managerial leadership, where the literature is full of broad generalizations supported by relatively little evidence. The supreme example of this generalization is the widely shared belief that democratic or participative leadership is the most effective leadership in nearly all circumstances. Until quite recently this view received little challenge, except in two rather ineffective forms which are very typical of the universalist dilemma.

Firstly when there is a poor match between prediction and result, as often happens in leadership studies (and also in studies of intelligence), one finds a plethora of caveats, usually in footnotes, about the special circumstances or particular situations which account for a given result (Fleishman *et al.*, 1955).

The second escape route is to talk about situational leadership in review articles and text books but without being able to specify the exact nature of the situation (Stogdill, 1948; Gibb, 1969). While the second escape route is more honest than the first, and incidentally denies the universality principle, it does not really help since with rare exceptions (Terman, 1904; Bavelas, 1950; Fiedler, 1967) it fails to identify which leadership method goes with which situation. This leads to intellectual chaos and the pessimism of the "practical man" who is simply told that our psychological variable depends on a variety of unspecified circumstances. A more useful approach is that of Kay and Warr (1970) who have noted that the relationship between democratic leadership and organizational effectiveness may be discontinuous or curvilinear.

A more satisfactory alternative to universalism is to incorporate statements of relativity or contingency from the very beginning into hypotheses relating to occupational psychology. If such a relativity framework had been used to study managerial leadership 20 years ago, there would probably now be much more useful and more scientific knowledge about this subject (Fiedler, 1967; Heller, 1971, 1973; Vroom and Yetton, 1973). There is a link here also with boundary disputes. At least some of the most relevant situational variables to be considered as contingencies are environmental or organizational variables. The argument for the inclusion of these allegedly non-psychological factors has only recently been put forward with some conviction (Inkson *et al.*, 1967; Pugh, 1969; Kay and Warr, 1970; Heller, 1976).

One of the more regrettable consequences of scientism is its influence on priorities in relation to research methods. There are two priorities we get wrong. Firstly we sometimes choose a method because in the hierarchy of scientific respectability it lies on top of the pile. Having chosen the method we then attack our problem — or worse still, we look round for a suitable problem upon which to practise our method. The second mistaken priority relates to our division of time and effort on data collection and data analysis. The true scientist, it is thought, spends most of his resources on sophisticated data analysis rather than on the task of getting good quality data. This has led us to neglect the potential of "Action research" (Heller, 1970; Town, 1973; Clark, 1976; Susman and Evered, 1978; Warr *et al.*, 1978) and to insufficient experimentation with longitudinal field studies (Witte, 1972; Pettigrew, 1973; Kimberley, 1976; Heller *et al.*, 1977; Combey, 1980).

The opposition to scientism has been growing over the last decade. In an important paper, Meehl (1967) has argued that increasing the power of statistical designs, other factors remaining equal, will enormously increase the probability of getting a large number of statistically significant but nonsensical results. Using a different logic, Argyris (1968) has repeatedly warned us about the unintended consequences of rigorous research; he has described occasions when subjects react to our apparently precise instruments by giving invalid information. The analysis of questionnaire data by means of Group Feedback Analysis supports this contention (Heller, 1969, 1971). Substantial recent support for a major re-assessment of appropriate research methodology in opposition to traditional positivistic preferences has come from a series of articles in the *Administrative Science Quarterly* edited by John Van Maanen (1979, 24).

We have to be aware of the danger from "back lash". Social scientists or their clients, who are disillusioned with the triviality or irrelevance of research findings based on scientism, may oppose research instruments of all kinds and take refuge in case studies, phenomenology or ethnomethodology (Douglas, 1971; Filmer *et al.*, 1972; Brown, 1973). The unreasonableness of this pendulum swing has been pointed out in different ways be Goldthorpe (1973), Phillips (1973), Bass (1974), Merrick (1975) and Dubin (1977), but needs much further detailed analysis.

C.   Compulsive causality

A closely related issue to scientism is compulsive causality. Two propositions are suggested:

i. In practice we do not have conclusive evidence of causal relationships in the major areas of our work and we are unlikely to have such evidence in the foreseeable future.

ii. We *do not need* causality to be scientific or practical; and we do not need causality in order to predict.

The objective of these propositions is to make a practical rather than a theoretical point. As long as changes in dependent variables are claimed to be the direct consequences of changes in the independent variable we invite at least four undesirable and unnecessary consequences:

1. We raise expectations about the existence of psychological laws which will give us evidence relating not only to sufficient but also to the necessary conditions leading to the occurrence of outcomes. Being unable to satisfy these conditions, we tend to be dissatisfied with ourselves and become defensive *vis-à-vis* our public.

2. We may be tempted to use inappropriate statistical methods and research designs, for instance, correlations and regression analysis where distribution-free non-parametric methods would correspond more closely with the reality of the data. The difficulty can be illustrated by looking at the work of a very influential school of psychology. In order to prove that participatory management is a causal variable, Likert at the University of Michigan (Likert, 1967, Chapter 5) adopted longitudinal studies. However, the work carried out within this research framework does not measure or control other relevant variables and consequently strains our credulity when causal interpretations are made (Marrow *et al.*, 1967).

3. To make it relatively easy for causal assumptions to be made, we tend to use a few variables at one time. For instance, we measure the impact of a particular training programme, of a particular test, of a defined and limited ergonomic variable, and so on. The failure of the Western Electric experiments at Hawthorne were not an adequate warning to us, but we became more conscious of the limitation of the single variable approach with the failure of job satisfaction and morale studies to predict increased output (Brayfield and Crockett, 1955). The unreality of this approach has received detailed criticism from Argyris (1968, 1976) and Warr and Wall (1975).

4. To facilitate causal attribution we need a hard criterion variable

of success or failure. As long as we take output or productivity measures we tend to confine our occupational psychology to the shop floor or the foreman level, or to laboratory studies, because this is where hard output measures can be obtained. Any review of literature during the last 50 years will confirm that this is in fact what has happened.

It is strange that we have worshipped causality for so long when most methodologists and physical scientists have given it up long ago. Popper sums up the position well when he says that "no kind of determinism, whether it be expressed as a principle of the uniformity of nature or as a law of universal causation, can be considered any longer a necessary assumption of scientific method; for physics, the most advanced of all sciences, has shown not only that it can do without such assumptions, but also that to some extent it contradicts them. Determinism is not a necessary prerequisite of a science which can make predictions" (Popper, 1945, Vol. 2, pp. 81; see also Kaufmann, 1944, p. 94; Bridgeman, 1960; Kahn and Weiner, 1967, p. 20). As psychologists we should also remember that Karl Pearson in his 1892 "Grammar of Science" suggested that correlations are an adequate substitute for causality.

D.   In defence of subjectivity

Finally there is our "subjectivity phobia", which is a derivative of scientism. Of course objective data should be obtained when they are relevant, but the problem is that the word subjective has today a distinctly pejorative meaning and this leads to all manner of difficulties.

If we want to know what people do at work it is clearly best to study their behaviour even if this is time-absorbing (Beishon and Palmer, 1972). But there are many areas of legitimate concern for us where behavioural indices or observation do not apply. The psychology of expectations is one such area and probably one of the most important as well as one of the more neglected. Duncan (1972) is one of the few British psychologists who has worked in this field and has rightly chided economists for omitting this variable from their hypotheses. Expectations are of critical importance in all investigations on incentives, work satisfaction, alienation, performance appraisal, vocational guidance, market research, leadership and organizational change to name just a few that come to mind readily. Subjectivity is the very essence of expectation, and if we could assess it we would probably find it to be one of the most powerful predictors of behaviour.

What people feel is important in all aspects of life including work, and some of the most intractable problems of the 1970s revolve around subjective psychological indices such as feelings about the quality of working life, social justice, and ethical standards (Bannister, 1973; Warr, 1973; Davis and Cherns, 1976). A major difficulty with these variables is not that they are subjective but that appropriate methods for assessing judgements and values of all kinds have yet to be devised.

The failure of subjective variables is often due to what Kaplan has called the "law of the instrument" (Kaplan, 1964, p. 28), i.e. our tendency to use the same instrument irrespective of the situation and therefore inappropriately. The weakest instrument for assessing complex value-laden subjective variables is the questionnaire, particularly the distributed questionnaire. This point was made very clearly by Mary Speak in her chairman's address to the Occupational Psychology Section (Speak, 1967).

As a final example consider the field of decision making. The objective aspects of decision making preoccupied economists and other social scientists for many years, although Bernouilli had put forward the notion of subjective value as long ago as 1738. But it was only with Herbert Simon that the scientific case against the rational model of man as a decision maker was convincingly made both on the theoretical and on the empirical level (Simon, 1945, 1959).

It was Simon who insisted on using the concepts "expectations", "psychic income" and "subjective environment" and who showed quite convincingly that managers do not try to achieve maximum profits, but adopt a subjective preference for a satisfactory return on capital employed. Simon also wondered how psychology and economics have got along with so little attention to each other for so many years. In his presidential address to the British Psychological Society, Audley reinforced these doubts and gave many examples of controlled experiments leading to an adequate mathematical conceptualization of subjective decision making processes, showing also that human satisfactions are more easily assessed by subjective values than by objective reality (Audley, 1970).

The four problems set out above are highly interdependent. In particular it seems that if we try to be scientific, by what we imagine to be the standards of science, then we will continue to draw tight boundaries to separate off traditional subjects. However, if we want social science to solve problems out there in the real world we cannot afford to impose our time honoured, but somewhat artificial, division of disciplines on this real world without distorting it significantly. The consequence of scientific standards and social relevance should be positively sought if we wish to develop a practical psychology of work which can cope with rapid and possibly discontinuous changes in our society.

References

ARGYRIS, C. (1968). Some unintended consequences of rigorous research. *Psychological Bulletin,* **70**, 185-197.

ARGYRIS, C. (1976). Problems and new directions in industrial psychology. In *Handbook of Industrial and Organizational Psychology* (Dunnette, M. D., ed.), Rand McNally, Chicago.

AUDLEY, R. (1970). Choosing. *Bulletin of the British Psychological Society,* **23**, 177-191.

BANNISTER, D. (1973). The shaping of things to come. *Bulletin of the British Psychological Society,* **26**, 293-295.

BASS, B. (1974). The substance and the shadow. *American Psychologist,* **29**, 870-886.

BAVELAS, A. (1950). Communication patterns in task-oriented groups. *Journal of the Accoustical Society of America,* **22**, 725-730.

BEISHON, R. J. AND PALMER, A. W. (1972). Studying managerial behaviour. *International Studies of Management and Organization,* **2**, 38-64.

BELL, D. (1976). *The Coming of Post-Industrial Society: A Venture in Social Forecasting.* Penguin Books, Harmondsworth.

BRAYFIELD, A. H. AND CROCKETT, W. H. (1955). Employee attitudes and employee performance, *Psychological Bulletin,* **52**, 396-424.

BRIDGEMAN, P. W. (1960, first published 1927). *The Logic of Modern Physics,* Macmillan, New York.

BROWN, G. W. (1973). Some thoughts on grounded theory. *Sociology,* **7**, 1-16.

CLARK, A. W. (1976). *Experimenting with Organizational Life: The Action Research Approach.* Plenum Press, New York.

COMBEY, P. (1980). A tracer approach to the study of organizations. *Journal of Management Studies,* **17**, 96-126.

DAVIS, L. AND CHERNS, A. (eds) (1976). *The Quality of Working Life* (2 volumes). Free Press, New York.

DOUGLAS, J. (ed.) (1971). *Understanding Everyday Life: Towards a Reconstruction of Sociological Knowledge.* Routledge & Kegan Paul, London.

DRUCKER, P. (1968). *The Age of Discontinuity: Guidelines to our Changing Society.* Pan Piper Books, London.

DUBIN, R. (1977). Theory building in applied areas. In *Handbook of Industrial and Organizational Psychology* (Dunnette, M. D., ed.). Rand McNally, Chicago.

DUNCAN, D. (1972). The economic significance of occupational psychology. Chairman's address to the British Psychological Society Occupational Psychology Section Conference, Warwick University.

EMERY, F. E. AND TRIST, E. L. (1973). *Towards A Social Ecology.* Plenum Press, London.

FIEDLER, F. E. (1967). *A Theory of Leadership Effectiveness.* McGraw Hill, New York.

FILMER, P., PHILLIPSON, M. I., SILVERMAN, D. AND WALSH, D. (1972). *New Directions in Sociological Theory,* Collier-Macmillan, London.

FLEISHMAN, E., HARRIS, E. AND BURTT, H. (1955). Leadership and supervision in industry. Ohio State University Educational Research Monograph No. 33.

GIBB, C. A. (1969). *Leadership.* Penguin, Harmondsworth.

GOLDTHORPE, J. (1973). A revolution in sociology. *Sociology,* 7, 449–462.

HELLER, F. A. (1969). Group feed-back analysis: A method of field research. *Psychological Bulletin,* 72, 108–117.

HELLER, F. A. (1970). Group feed-back analysis as a change agent. *Human Relations,* 23, 319–333.

HELLER, F. A. (1971). *Managerial Decision Making: A study of Leadership Styles and Power Sharing Among Senior Managers.* Tavistock, London.

HELLER, F. A. (1973). Leadership, decision-making and contingency theory. *Industrial Relations,* 12, 183–199.

HELLER, F. A. (1976). Decision processes: An analysis of power-sharing at senior organizational levels. In *Handbook of Work, Organization and Society* (Dubin, R., ed.). Rand McNally, Chicago.

HELLER, F. A., DRENTH, P. J. D., KOOPMAN, P. AND RUS, V. (1977). A longitudinal study in participative decision-making. *Human Relations,* 30, 567–587.

HIRSCH, F. (1977). *Social Limits to Growth.* Routledge & Kegan Paul, London.

INKSON, J. H. K., PAYNE, R. L. AND PUGH, D. S. (1967). Extending the occupational environment. *Occupational Psychology,* 41, 35–47.

KAHN, H. AND WEINER, A. J. (1967). *The Year 2000.* Macmillan, London.

KAPLAN, A. (1964). *The Conduct of Enquiry: Methodology for Behavioral Science.* Chandler, San Francisco.

KAUFMAN, F. (1944). *Methodology of the Social Sciences.* Oxford University Press, London.

KAY, H. AND WARR, P. (1970). Some future developments in occupational psychology. *Occupational Psychology,* 44, 293–301.

KERR, C. AND ROSOW, J. (eds) (1979). *Work in America: The Decade Ahead.* Van Nostrand Reinhold, Wokingham, Berkshire.

KIMBERLEY, J. R. (1976). Some issues in longitudinal organizational research. *Sociological Methods and Research,* 4, 321-346.

LIKERT, R. (1967). *The Human Organization.* McGraw Hill, New York.

MANKIN, D. (1978). *Towards a Post-Industrial Psychology: Emerging Perspectives on Technology, Work, Education and Leisure.* John Wiley, New York.

MARROW, A. J., BOWERS, D. G. AND SEASHORE, S. E. (1967). *Management by Participation.* Harper & Row, New York.

MEEHL, P. (1967). Theory testing in psychology and physics. *Philosophy of Science,* 34, 103-115.

MERRICK, S. (1975). The standard problem: Meaning and values in measurement and evaluation. *American Psychologist,* 30, 955-966.

OPPENHEIMER, R. (1956). Analogy in science. *American Psychologist,* 11, 127-135.

PETTIGREW, A. M. (1973). *The Politics of Organizational Decision-Making,* Tavistock, London.

PHILLIPS, D. (1973). *Abandoning Method.* Jossey Bass, San Francisco.

POPPER, K. R. (1945). *The Open Society and Its Enemies,* vols. 1 and 2. Routledge & Kegan Paul, London.

POPPER, K. R. (1957). *The Poverty of Historicism.* Routledge & Kegan Paul, London.

PUGH, D. S. (1969). Organizational behaviour: An approach from psychology. *Human Relations,* 22, 345-354.

ROGERS, C. R. (1973). Some new challenges. *American Psychologist,* 28, 379-387.

SIMON, H. A. (1945). *Administrative Behavior.* Macmillan, New York.

SIMON, H. A. (1959). Theories of decision making in economics and behavioral science. *American Economic Review,* 49, 253-283.

SPEAK, M. (1967). Communication failure in questioning. *Occupational Psychology,* 41, 169-179.

STOGDILL, R. M. (1948). Personal factors associated with leadership: A survey of the literature. *Journal of Psychology,* 25, 35-71.

SUSMAN, G. AND EVERED, R. D. (1978). An assessment of the scientific merit of action research. *Administrative Science Quarterly,* 23, 582-603.

TERMAN, L. M. (1904). A preliminary study of the psychology and pedagogy of leadership. *Journal of Genetic Psychology,* 11, 413-451.

TOFFLER, A. (1970). *Future Shock.* Bantam, New York.

TOWN, S. (1973). Action research and social policy: Some recent British experience. *Sociological Review,* 21, 573-598.

VAN MAANEN, J. (1979). Reclaiming qualitative methods for organizational research. *Administrative Science Quarterly,* 24, 520-526.

VROOM, V. AND YETTON, P. (1973). *Leadership and Decision Making.* University of Pittsburgh, Pennsylvania.

WARR, P. (1973). Towards a more human psychology. *Bulletin of the British Psychological Society*, **26**, 1-7.

WARR, P. AND WALL, T. (1975). *Work and Well-Being*, Penguin, Harmondsworth.

WARR, P., FINEMAN, S., NICHOLSON, N. AND PAYNE, R. (1978). *Developing Employee Relations.* Saxon House and Gower Press, Farnborough, Hampshire.

WITTE, E. (1972). Field research on complex decision-making processes: The phase theorem. *International Studies of Management and Organization*, **2**, 156-182.

14 Taylorism Today and
its Contradictions

MAURICE DE MONTMOLLIN

Why include a discussion on Taylorism in a book devoted to work psychology? It could be argued that Taylorism is an old ideology and an old technology, interesting to no one but the historian, or the mechanical engineer, but not to the social scientist. On the contrary, the opinion advanced here is that Taylorism is alive as an ideology and even as a technology. Taylorism is the implicit ideology of people who, even if they are young, have to work in organizations which were conceived and implemented by managers, engineers and scientists who were educated in the twenties and the thirties when Taylorism was predominant. The principles of rationalization advocated by Taylor and his followers continue to be implemented in offices and factories by many who may not even have heard of "scientific management". If you are not convinced, you should walk around the shopfloor of any factory, anywhere, West or East.

Social scientists, particularly work psychologists, also share this ideology, even if they have never read Taylor. As a result there are provoking contradictions, not only due to the development of Taylorism itself, but also arising from conflicts with others' ideologies, especially the humanistic one, subscribed to by most psychologists.

In this chapter, Tayloristic ideology will be characterized by three linked concepts: Work division, Science, and Order.

A.   Work division

Work division into the smallest manageable units is perhaps Taylor's main innovation, i.e. the rationalization of production. The scrupulous distinction between management and execution was revolutionary because, until then, complexity and craftsmanship were seen as inextricably linked with the organization of work in which every worker was technically his own manager. What Taylor did was to introduce the modern "expert". This individual is supposed to know about work and the workers, although not himself a part of the main work force. The workers themselves were presumed to be ignorant on these matters.

This view is still in existence among social scientists as well as among engineers. Industrial psychologists assume they know more about the aptitudes and skills of workers than the workers do themselves. They consider themselves experts who can say who is able to do what. Similarly, training specialists think they know better how to teach trainees than trainees know how to learn; ergonomists to know more about the mental load of tired operators than the latter, and social psychologists to know how to motivate foremen, who may not have heard of "motivation". In the same vein, organizational psychologists are supposed to know a lot of things about leadership, of which the leaders themselves are absolutely unaware. Work psychology is a complex and very wide domain, which needs a lot of specialized academic training. The serious nature of the subject can be seen from the *Handbook of Industrial and Organizational Psychology* edited by Dunnette (1976). It is just a handbook, in which the main topics are summarized: but they occupy 1740 large pages.

Let us assume that work psychologists are experts. Where then is the contradiction? It occurs because the humanistic ideology, which is very popular at the present time, conflicts with the Tayloristic one. When psychologists try to promote "industrial democracy", "participation", "autonomy", "Quality of Working Life" they find they cannot force someone to be more autonomous, more involved in his job, more "human". For example, experts in job enrichment are frequently disappointed to find that workers accept such programmes only as willingly as, in France, the geese are "fattened for their livers". So there is the contradiction that so-called "humanistic" psychologists have to be humanistic both for themselves and for the workers who are the objects of their humanization programmes.

This contradiction is not a superficial one. We have to be experts. We are work psychologists, not some non-directive clinical psychologists, who have nothing to do but to listen to their clients. We have something to say, and perhaps it is of interest to the workers. But we also know perfectly well that workers — even the unskilled ones — are less and less prepared to be guided like little children by their teachers.

Of course, one can escape this contradiction. For example, one can, simply, be an expert in work psychology without doubting the acceptability of one's proposal. One can ensure that communication is only from expert to expert, which is a lot more pleasant. But it is (or should be) a subject of deep concern to work psychologists that never, and nowhere, do ordinary workers (the "non-experts") seem to be interested in work psychology. Indeed, in some quarters, they show active opposition to it.

B. Science

It is widely believed that experts are experts only if they are scientists. Science thus legitimates the domination of the "scientific manager". Taylor reflected the pre-eminence of science, not only in the domain of the engineer, but also in the social sciences. From this perspective, psychology, sociology, physiology, have to be scientific if they are to be recognized and accepted as applied disciplines, a position which has its merits and few would doubt that we must strive in this direction. Without a scientific basis, there is constant danger that work psychology is reduced to magical manipulations, superstitious practices and to dogmatic stupidities, as seen in transactional analysis, graphology, or characterologies.

Where is the contradiction here? Simply that scientific work psychology has not been successful. Even in the early days of work study, the trivial "time" shown by the stopwatch was inaccurate, and inapplicable without some (important) local empirical adjustment. This is even more true of the highly sophisticated methodology of modern social scientists.

In selection, tests, mental or otherwise, are unable to predict precisely and consistently the success of "scientifically" selected workers. The problem is extremely complex — and the use of tests, in some parts of Europe, seems to be declining. New training procedures, such as programmed learning, have not proved more efficient than the old ones, such as the teacher with his blackboard. Theoretically, they should be more efficient, but something seems to limit the generalization of their application. Theories of motivation are numerous, and ingenious, but no one has succeeded in motivating workers with no motivation to be motivated. Which psychologist has really changed something important in one organization?

Problems of this kind, which are well known but rarely acknowledged among members of the profession, are the main reason for the gap between theory and practice. They also account for the extremely rare empirical validations in work psychology. Perhaps the strange feature of handbooks of work psychology in which the examples given are almost always "simplified", or even invented, can be traced to this source.

Is this too pessimistic? It is to be hoped so. But these serious difficulties show the contradictions in the domain between a scientific approach and practical implementation. They are not arguments for a condemnation. Perhaps the contradiction can never be fully resolved but we have no choice but to try to resolve it. There is, fortunately, from time to time some limited conquest (by the neo-behaviouristic troops, for instance) showing some advance in the field. Maybe, as Sylvia Shimmin says: "One reason for this is that many of the problems in which psychologists are interested . . . come into the category identified by Garrett Hardin the biologist, as those for which there is no technical solution . . ." (Shimmin, 1978.) But the absence of a technical solution should not mean the absence of a technical approach!

Confronted by this contradiction, some work psychologists try to escape it, through hard work, perseverance, and social influence: they become professors of work psychology. This is a clever solution: if one cannot solve the contradictions between a scientific approach and the life of organizations one retreats into teaching the science to those who will be in charge of its implementation. To be both a scientist and a practitioner is too difficult, at least in Europe. This was exemplified at the last International Congress of Applied Psychology (Munich, July 1978), where the large majority of the papers were presented by professors who had not themselves achieved the interesting things they described.

C. Order

Order and law were also very important to Taylor. Implicit in any claim to the scientific study of work is the belief in orderliness and the possibility of structuring organizations on some rational basis. It is felt that there ought to be some natural order which, when implemented, precludes the possibility of conflicts. Consequently the Tayloristic ideology is also a bureaucratic one. Rules are better than improvised adaptation, and uncertainty must, and can, be removed. Considering order, the Tayloristic ideology produces today both a minor and a major contradiction for work psychologists. The minor contradiction is found in the belief that it is possible to construct a taxonomy of jobs, on the one hand, and of the attributes of people, on the other, thus enabling a perfect match to be made between the two. This is the underlying belief of selection procedures and of the notion of "the right man in the right place" as a consequence of the division of work.

Of course, industrial psychologists have made the genuine Tayloristic model a little more sophisticated. There are now many aptitudes, abilities, and skills, corresponding to many tasks and jobs. The contradiction is, as is well-known, that this correspondence is more and more fanciful, and therefore that the professional activity of the selection psychologists (that is still the majority of work psychologists in Europe) becomes more and more ritualistic. It is very unusual, in the real professional life of psychologists, that validity coefficients are calculated. And this is good: when calculated they rarely reach the 0·40 level. In reality, people, and jobs, are evolving in changing organizations; but this is ignored by the expert in selection (see Montmollin, 1972).

The major contradiction results from the reality of conflict in the world of work. If this world were essentially ordered, it would follow that there is no place in it for conflict. Or, more precisely, conflict would only arise from superficial misunderstanding, or sometimes from defiance of the "natural" laws. So, any conflict would soon disappear if more attention were given, say, to education and supervision. Taylor himself argued that scientific management would make strikes impossible. Similarly, there should be no need of any bargaining: one cannot, indeed, bargain scientific data. In other words, Tayloristic ideology denies the existence of conflict, today as well as yesterday.

But the facts are difficult to refute: there is always a lot of conflict in organizations. Thus work psychologists — especially "organizational psychologists" — are constantly confronted with conflicting interests, e.g. between managers who want more productivity and workers who want more security, or between managers who want more efficiency and workers who want more money. Work psychologists approach these conflicts with courage and hope, if not always with confidence. The first tactic they use is (or was, since it is no longer in fashion) to deny that the conflict is an organizational one, and reduce it to the "psychological" inter-individual level, which is relatively easy to solve. Another tactic is to support one of the parties to the conflict (usually the party which pays the psychologist), and help it to win the battle. This is the position adopted by psychologists in some big American companies. In Europe, where conflicts are more or less endemic, work psychologists seldom take up such an overt partisan position. If one were to take sides in this way, it would give too much reality to the conflict; it would mean becoming a soldier in the battle, thereby acknowledging the existence of the war, which is "disorder".

It is not easy to escape this contradiction. Taylorism is contested by the humanistic experts, who are seen by workers as representing a new gadget in management techniques. Yugoslavian self-management turns into bureaucracy; Kibbutzim cannot escape elitism; and the Maoïstic attempt to destroy the difference between workers and experts is now considered to be the criminal madness of the Gang of Four.

European work psychologists see themselves as "go-betweens", or facilitators of communication. They are trained to cope with processes, not with contents; to be "change agents", without too much consideration as to the direction of the change. In this way they deny the existence of conflict. They attempt to bring reason, to help people realize that conflicts are irrational. Located between opposing groups, they are in the middle — or maybe even above? — isolated, hoping not to be perceived as bosses by the workers, and nevertheless hoping to be considered as experts by the bosses. Although they refuse to let others have conflicts, they succeed in keeping the contradictions to themselves.

References

DE MONTMOLLIN, M. (1972). *Les Psychopitres. Une Autocritique de la Psychologie Industrielle.* P.U.F., Paris.

SHIMMIN, S. (1978). Applying psychology in organisations. Paper presented at the XIX International Congress of Applied Psychology, Munich, July 30 - August 5, 1978.

15 Work Psychology as a Conflict-centred Technology

ENZO SPALTRO

The view advanced in this Chapter is that conflict is central to the work situation and therefore that work psychology should be seen as a technology focusing on conflict. This follows from a definition of work as effort to achieve advantages, and the assumption that everybody involved tries to minimize the costs to themselves and to maximize the advantages. Since participants in the work process are many, there are also many points of view about the effects and advantages entailed. What is an advantage to some is a cost to others. Therefore the working situation is always a conflicting situation. This is the basic situation faced by anyone who wants to understand the perceptions and feelings of people in employment. Associated with work conflict are certain concepts. The first is the notion of "preventive violence", i.e. taking strong action to prevent the oppression of others, motivated by a fear of being oppressed oneself.

Closely associated with this view is the notion of fighting, which has a double meaning. One can fight for something or fight against a course of action. In other words, fighting can be centred on ourselves, or it may be centred on others.

Yet another concept inherent in the psychology of conflict is pluralism, i.e. the multiple interpretation which may be given of a particular situation or issue.

It follows from this that, in dealing with work situations, we have to see that fighting is not a pathology, but a normal way of coping with and living between the boundaries of controlled aggression. It is the quality of fighting and not its presence which allows us to appreciate the nature of a work situation and organization. Fighting for something is better than fighting against somebody; creativity is better than preventive action, and pluralism is a more realistic view than a unitary approach to diagnosis and intervention.

In using the expression "work psychology" we should recognize that two possible relationships are involved. The first puts work at the centre and psychology at the periphery, while the second puts psychology at the core, and work at the periphery. This duality of meaning, which may underlie the simple term "work psychology", represents an inherent contradiction between what I call "the work of psychology" and "the psychology of work". The latter, that is the psychology of work, is conceivable as a desirable, technological possibility, which reflects the hope of bringing about a better world. "The work of psychology" tends to be thought of in terms of professional duties and responsibilities, i.e. in terms of regulation, rather than revelation.

One consequence of this is that some industrial and organizational psychologists in Italy do not wish to declare themselves as professional psychologists because of the repressive dimension of "the work of psychology". They use psychological techniques but they do not declare themselves as psychologists.

In work situations some people seek to over-emphasize subjectivity and others objectivity. Usually people with power tend to describe objectivity as scientific, good, rational, trustworthy and useful, whereas subjectivity is seen as arbitrary, unreliable, unreal and dangerous. People without power, on the other hand, whose aim is to minimize their effort and to increase their advantages in the work situation, tend to equate subjectivity with freedom, reality, humanity and utility. They regard objectivity as representative of imposition, formality, abstraction and superficiality.

Industrial and organizational psychologists need to recognize these conflicting views and the different perceptions of powerful and powerless people. Although they consider themselves experts in the subjective life of workers, they should beware of over-emphasizing subjectivity. Since psychologists themselves may be repressed, they may, without knowing it, try to repress others.

A major contradiction in the field of work psychology is that it is just when the study of conflict is most needed that it is the most difficult to undertake. We must avoid considering the work situation as favourable to psychology and to an open-minded appreciation of subjective factors. As conflicts grow, psychologists have increasing difficulties in finding effective means of intervention and they are forced to abandon their traditional frames of reference, theories and classical approaches. All parties to work conflict have their points of view, which have their validity, and must be treated with equal respect by the work psychologists. This means that they are forced to renounce the unidimensional approach of "science" and orthodox methodology, and take account of the subjective origins of these different attitudes. For many psychologists it is threatening to relinquish scientific practices as it gives them a feeling of losing their professional identity.

This dilemma, that is of how to deal with these findings and their consequences, is now the basic problem for industrial and organizational psychologists in Italy, who want to deal professionally with the quality of work and the quality of life. Being able to treat conflict appears to be the main professional goal for today's industrial psychologists.

In trying to construct a conflict-centred psychology one should take account of a number of basic assumptions. These include:

a. The transition of a unitary to a pluralistic approach entails a change in the power bases within organizations. The sharing of leadership functions means that you can have more than one cock in a poultry-yard! (Italian proverb)

b. Conflict is as essential for organizations as arousal is for individuals. Under-arousal leads to passivity, and over-arousal to paralysis. Similarly an organization without conflict is inactive, and one with too much conflict is unable to function. Thus, using conflict effectively should be the goal of organizational psychology.

c. Work relationships are constantly being renewed, changed, projected and realized. So there is always scope for social exploration and experimentation in the work situation. One should not assume that work relationships are fixed.

d. Every worker is a complex individual, and therefore there is an infinity of ways in which people may feel useful or discounted in their work.

e. Participation entails fighting to belong to some group, that is, without the existence of groups in which membership is desired and for which people will fight to belong true participation is impossible.

A conflict centred work psychology is likely to concentrate on the following issues:

a. Changing attitudes towards conflict and people's reactions to it.

b. Training personnel such as supervisors, managers, mediators, negotiators in the use of a theoretical model incorporating not only the values of the dominant culture (managers) but also of the subordinate culture (workers).

c. Design and redesign of working groups within the context of human factor engineering (ergonomics) and also the extension of this approach to man–machine systems and man–environment systems.

d. An approach to accident prevention and safety, which concentrates on organizational design and organizational climate, as much as on technical aspects of safe working.

e. Training people how to recognize social conflict originating in the work situation which has not been identified and treated, but denied and refused.

f. Process consultation, which takes account of the dynamics of work relationships as well as their content; acting as a process-consultant is one of the most promising areas of application of a conflict-based psychology.

If these trends become established some future dimensions of work psychology will be:

a. The developments of special concepts and techniques to deal with conflict, such as contradiction analysis.

b. An extension of the interface concept to facilitate understanding of the passage from one culture to another, and the acceleration of this process.

c. Much work on the measurement of power and leadership, with particular reference to the problem of conflicting leadership, i.e. of dealing with two or more sources of legitimacy and their influence on work dynamics.

d. The development of a dialectic approach to the study of power, and the exploration of its several meanings.

e. The development of a new concept of efficiency of work, taking account of psychological factors, such as the ratio of human cost to organizational results.

f. Development of a new role for psychologists as analysers of inter-group as well as intra-group relations, including emphasis on feedback, "coaching" and action research.

In my view, organizations are increasingly to be considered as clients, with problems of health, illness, hygiene and therapy. Associated with this are the notions of psychological "pollution" within organizations and an organizational "ecology" in the wider environment. Using these concepts facilitates training in the more effective deployment of psychological resources in work situations.

16 Challenges of Diversity: An American's View of Work Psychology in Europe

MILTON D. HAKEL

Europe presents a marvellous and often bewildering diversity of forms, ideas and institutions. What I attempt to do here is to survey some of the challenges to work psychologists presented by that diversity from the perspective of a non-European. But first let me state my credentials. I am well acquainted with the editors of this volume, having worked with them since 1974, first in drafting a review article which was published in *Personnel Psychology* (de Wolff and Shimmin, 1976) and then in discussing the issues presented in this book. I have travelled extensively in Europe, and have attended several international conventions. In 1978 I spent over four months in Italy conducting research on the influences of political ideologies on organizational staffing, supported by a Fulbright–Hays Research Award. From these experiences, plus my editorship of the research journal *Personnel Psychology* and extensive reading, the following observations are offered.

After describing the general social context within which European work psychology is developing, I review several factors which I see as aiding the development of work psychology in Europe. Factors which are hindering this development are then examined. In conclusion the advantages of informal, multinational peer groups are stressed.

A.   Europe as context

There are 28 countries in Europe, covering 7% of the Earth's land area, where 18% of the world's people live. The languages spoken are numerous and, when dialects and regional variations are counted, linguistic diversity is very great. As a result, communications are bound to be difficult.

Although cultures, mores, and social norms vary dramatically between countries, and even within countries, supranational associations are now being formed (e.g. EEC). Family structure and traditional social roles are changing and, as in the USA, new conceptions of appropriate sex roles are emerging. Social legislation (the Equal Pay Act, the Equal Employment Opportunity Act, and the Equal Rights Amendment) concerning women's rights exemplifies these changes.

Social conflict is increasing as various groups seek liberation from varying kinds of oppression and oppressors. Religious, ethnic, racial, political and economic issues lie beneath these conflicts.

Governmental forms vary greatly, and diverse political ideologies are espoused, debated and practised. Relations between neighbouring governments range from friendship to open hostility. Economic ideologies are equally varied, ranging from *Laissez-faire* private capitalism to cooperativism to state capitalism. Mixes of these ideologies, such as state participation in private enterprise, are common. There are wide variations in levels of economic development, though even the poorest regions compare favourably with the rest of the world. Nevertheless, the distribution of wealth and standards of living vary greatly. Mass migrations of labour are influenced by unemployment, labour shortages, and rising expectations for material goods.

Mass media communication, "pop" culture in music and the arts, increasing trade, and increasing levels of education are creating greater interdependence among countries and regions, leading toward cultural homogenization.

Bitter historic animosities are being subordinated by the necessity to accommodate superordinate problems of conventional and nuclear energy use, world population growth, world food production, pollution, militarism and the nuclear "balance of terror", and geopolitics and world peace.

The context within which European psychologists work is diverse and changing. Can a scientific and professional discipline develop under such circumstances?

B. The positive aspects of diversity

As an applied social scientist, I was trained to be aware of the effects of "restriction of range" on the reliability of observation and measurement. While I intellectually appreciated this statistical fact, I did not appreciate it emotionally until I lived in another culture for several months, long enough to begin questioning many assumptions which I had previously taken for granted.

For example, in Italy I sought to study the relative importance of personal qualifications ("merit") and job applicant and potential employer similarity of economic–political opinions ("ideology") as influences on selection decisions. I assumed that research methods I had previously used could be translated and adapted successfully. I assumed that selection decisions are commonplace in large organizations. These were simple and superficial assumptions, quickly corrected by experience. But I also discovered I held some deeper assumptions that did not become evident until much later in my stay in Italy, e.g. that merit is a legitimate basis for allocating rewards, and that research *per se* is worth doing. These latter two items might be better described as values, and I found differences between these values and those of others. The differences were not expected, but they helped to make me more sensitive to the range of phenomena I saw.

I have not completely shed my "cultural blinkers" and I have not fully adapted to cultural relativity. Perhaps it is not possible to do so fully. However, I do see some of the boundaries and assumptions, and some of the cultural limitations, which act to restrict the range over which observations and measurements are made by work psychologists. American research on pay plans, incentives, motivation, job satisfaction, work group relations, union relations, interpersonal conflict, and leadership, influence and power may contain findings and theories appropriate for other countries and cultures, but in the end local empirical validation is needed. There is no area of practice or research, including the topics just listed, which could not be improved by studying the phenomenon over a greater range of variation.

Any enterprise, whether it be a manufacturing industry, a service organization, a government agency, or an association of volunteers, can be construed as a system created to achieve definable purposes. Comparative studies of the ways in which work is performed to achieve these purposes, both within and between cultures, is and will be useful in contributing to knowledge and practice. Comparability is best insured if it is delimited by commonality of purpose rather than commonality of process, product or context. For example, there are many variations among European countries in selection and staffing processes, and the best vantagepoint for studying these variations is given when the processes serve a common purpose.

Cross-cultural and cross-national research is difficult to do well, but it is worth doing well. While every subfield of industrial and organizational psychological research and practice can benefit from cross-national research, there are a few fields which European work psychologists will recognize as providing special opportunities of this kind:

a. Longitudinal studies of industrial democracy, in the many different forms in which that concept is practiced, are an obvious target of opportunity.

b. Participative decision making, participative management, team building, and other organizational development approaches are equally good targets, especially when studied cross-nationally.

c. Similarly, tests of competing theories can be conducted more powerfully, especially for the topics of motivation, satisfaction and leadership.

d. Conflict and conflict resolution can be analysed in many cultural contexts, for both individuals and groups.

e. Guest workers, their training and integration into developed societies and their selective migration from economically less-developed societies, constitute a particular opportunity.

Because of Europe's diversity, these are especially favourable areas in which to test the universality of many theories and assumptions.

These are obvious subjects because they are familiar to members of the profession and relatively accessible to cross-national research and development. Cultural and contextual diversity facilitates improved and unique approaches to them. However, my impression is that contact among European work psychologists is underdeveloped.

And there are also difficulties stemming from cultural diversity, which hinder the study of these topics. We turn to them now.

C. The difficult aspects of diversity

Anyone who is optimistic about the potential gains to be obtained from cross-national research will, upon beginning such research, soon discover the true and difficult challenges entailed, as I know to my cost.

Consider first the question of language. I have been privileged to be a member of a multinational peer group which includes the editors of this volume. It is an experience that I strongly recommend to everyone. The group has been a constant source of learning for me, but it has also demonstrated the difficulties of language. The group spoke English, which is the most common language for scientific communication in psychology. Nevertheless, this was a stumbling block, both for those to whom English is a second language and to those who speak no other tongue. Our meetings were exhausting for me, even though I was not burdened by having to speak a language other than my first. My fluency in Italian and French is poor, and I have been frustrated many times in trying to express a subtle nuance of a complex relationship, having only a limited vocabulary and grammar. Thus, I understand others' reluctance to incur the difficulties and the social risk of working and conversing in a second language.

Research funding is another problem. It is to be hoped that funding from national governmental agencies and from private organizations will soon be supplemented by international funding. However, this will require a much higher level of quasi-political activity than is typical of scholars, researchers and professionals. The likelihood of success is small. Possible sources of support such as the EEC, ILO and NATO have charters which limit the possible kinds of projects that they can support. Moreover, "national" interests usually take precedence over international ones.

In a related vein, new publication outlets are needed. Better communication should alleviate some of the difficulties caused by diversity in educational programmes and professional training. While national journals serve a much needed function, the challenge for the coming decades is to develop a genuine international exchange of information on research and practice, and not just in Europe. American psychologists' awareness of European developments is next to nil.

A more complex issue is national and ethnic chauvinism. National rivalries are well established and well reinforced. Especially between cultures there is a great potential for misinterpreting others' behaviours, leading to unneeded rivalry, aggressiveness and/or threats to self-esteem. Stereotyping is a related hindrance. Petty personal rivalries are as apt to happen within countries as between them, and in either case they are annoying at best and destructive at worst. Though competition is motivating, psychological research and practice is not a zero-sum game; nor is there an international league table. Overcoming the dysfunctional consequences of stereotyping and national and personal rivalries is a major challenge for European work psychologists.

Another difficulty is that of achieving a consensus about appropriate goals for work psychology. There are serious differences of opinion about the worth of scientific and technological development. Public scepticism about the desirability of technology is growing. In the United States, discussion concerning ethical issues in research and practice is at an all time high. The "servants of power" issue continues to generate a great deal of emotion. In recent years this debate has at least advanced beyond espousal of naive and Luddite exhortations to eschew power, and from simplistic left-wing, right-wing confrontations, to the examination of goals, social costs and social benefits. In this pluralistic setting, consensus is difficult to obtain. In the absence of consensus, however, fragmentation of research, demoralization, and public antipathy can be expected. Even a limited degree of consensus is worth achieving.

Perhaps the greatest problem is that of historical inertia. The coming decades will bring major social and technological changes, and yet many psychologists in Europe and the USA seem to be locked into social roles and sets of cultural expectations that prevent fully effective scientific and professional service. Selection specialists who continue to rely on unvalidated procedures illustrate this point.

But failure to keep up with changing circumstance is only part of the problem. Sponsor and client expectations change slowly. Again using selection as an example, few sponsors are aware of assessment centres and realistic job previews, and thus expect little innovation from the selection specialist. We are stereotyped by others, and reputations are difficult to establish and difficult to improve.

Questions debated in this volume concerning the optimal depth and breadth of specialization, the optimal permeability of boundaries between our field and other disciplines, and goals for the field deserve the scrutiny of every work psychologist. Comfortable, historically sanctioned roles will need to be updated to take advantage of the coming opportunities for contributions to knowledge and to human welfare.

D.   How to cope with these issues

I want to close this outsider's perspective on work psychology in Europe by elaborating a comment I have already made. It concerns the best means, short of long-term "total-immersion" exchanges, that I can see for coping with diverse goals, roles, expectations, problems and opportunities. This is through the establishment of international peer groups.

Meetings of such peer groups are an excellent vehicle for creating understanding and mutuality. Attending international meetings and conventions is a good beginning, but such meetings are not held with sufficient frequency to provide the needed continuity. Conventions are a good place, however, to meet people who might be stimulating members of a peer group. Preferably, the group itself should be organized around some specific purpose or task. My experience in several American groups as well as the European group suggests that the group should have 10–20 members to ensure sufficient attendance at meetings to generate diverse and spirited discussion.

Successful groups seldom have a formal leader or a fixed organizational scheme. Rather, all members participate fully in making policies and decisions concerning membership, discussion topics, and group activities. Meetings are usually held twice a year for one to three days, and group members take turns serving as host to organize the meeting. Needless to say, personal animosity and direct competition (for appointments, contracts, or other resources) are out of place in such a group, and for an international group everyone needs sufficient linguistic skill to preclude the need for professional translators. Informal peer groups cannot be established nor maintained by decree. Their success depends entirely on personal interest, goodwill, and mutual respect.

In my experience, there is no substitute for the continuous support and stimulation that develop in a peer group. It provides the setting for the information exchange, colleagueship and challenging of assumptions which, as indicated, are essential for the development of the profession. Furthermore, it serves to strengthen a sense of identity which transcends national differences and so facilitates international cooperation.

References

DE WOLFF, C. J. AND SHIMMIN, S. (1976). The psychology of work in Europe: A review of a profession. *Personnel Psychology,* **29**, 175–195.

Section 4
Future Trends

CHARLES J. DE WOLFF, SYLVIA SHIMMIN and
MAURICE DE MONTMOLLIN

17 The Future of Work Psychology

A. Introduction

Let us now attempt to draw together the main themes which have been discussed in this volume. We have seen how the history of work psychology in different countries shows some resemblances, but also quite clear differences. For example, industrial psychology gained academic respectability at quite an early stage of its development in Britain, but has not been given commensurate credence by industry. In Germany, on the other hand, there were well established centres of application and industrial support early on, but the subject is still under-represented in the academic world (McCollum, 1960). The situation in France is different again, with industrial and organizational psychology having little impact in either the academic or the industrial sphere. The contrasts between Italy and Poland are apparent from the papers from Spaltro and Dobrzyński in this book. Therefore, there is no such thing as a world-wide system of work psychology and, in looking to the future, no general prescription will be valid across all countries.

In this concluding chapter we want to consider what can be done to bring about a desirable future for work psychology, recognizing that there are no easy answers, and that future directions in each country will be shaped by both national and international events. It is our intention to show that there are several options, each having both positive and negative aspects, on the basis of which it may be possible to develop scenarios for the future. The scenarios outlined below are

those which the authors see as possible directions which work
psychology might take during the next decades. They are not
presented as predictions of what *will* happen, nor do they represent
mutually exclusive developments, but are a synopsis of possibilities
which we think can be discerned in the current situation in Europe.
Others may not agree with us and we should like to hear their views.
Our purpose is not to press our own interpretations, but to invite
members of the profession to take up discussion of these issues. In this
way, we believe, the chances of shaping the future can be considerably
enhanced.

B.   Laissez-faire

The first scenario is that of no change from the present, i.e. a situation
of *laissez-faire*, or free for all, in which market forces, individual
entrepreneurs, government policies and similar factors interact
indiscriminately. This is the future which is often taken for granted. It
is also frequently justified by such notions as "let a hundred flowers
blossom" and the view that genius cannot be cultivated in a systematic
way, a viewpoint which bears the marks of both Darwinian and
probability theories. Furthermore, it has great appeal in that it is easy
to envisage, it displeases no one in the profession and allows each
individual to continue his or her present activities unchallenged. The
advantage of this scenario is that, confronted with a turbulent
environment which there is no known way of handling, it does not lead
to any premature closing of options. In theory, at any rate, flexibility is
maintained, and innovations are assumed to stand an equal chance of
being accepted or rejected. The underlying philosophy resembles that
of the British concept of "muddling through" and is believed to have
survival value.

On the negative side, it is possible to discern a number of
disadvantages. There is a risk that people will feel that no one is in
control and consequently will experience considerable anxiety. In the
long run, there may be much frustration in the profession because
there is no well-defined system ordering activities such as education,
training, application and career development. It seems to us that the
tendency of psychologists to work on an individual basis is likely to be
furthered under these circumstances, with associated lack of

professional support and organization. The result may be an overlapping of activities within the profession and with other disciplines, leading to confusion on the part of clients and sponsors.

Another consequence is that quality control may become even more difficult than it is at present. Currently such control is exercised largely through the system of academic refereeing of papers, journal articles and so on, as well as through the personal recommendations of practitioners. Although we do not advocate institutional controls, which can become dysfunctional, without a strong professional organization and well-defined domain, colleague surveillance and sanctions against unacceptable practice are impossible. Likewise, clients lack an advisory body or a source of information as to what they may legitimately expect from psychologists.

Diversification of effort also means that expertise is spread thinly over a number of activities and that concentrated action is rare. Even today it is common to find major research programmes being undertaken by only two or three people, as a result of diversification of interests and activities. Similarly, there are teaching institutions which have only a single work psychologist on their staff, in order to be able to include this subject in their curricula. The situation can easily develop where it becomes impossible to identify the boundaries of the domain at all and, furthermore, the field becomes more vulnerable to distortions by fads and fashion.

C. Reform from within

By the term "reform from within" we mean restructuring and reorganization within the profession of psychology as a whole, which will give more opportunities to work psychologists to develop their own lines of interest, while remaining within the total domain of psychology.

Two possible lines of development are outlined below which we think could occur, but we would not claim these are the only ones.

The first would entail more formal distinction being made between scientific work and application, and perhaps even a separation between the two in training programmes and in branches of the professional organization. There is a long-standing debate on this issue and a history of role ambiguity experienced by work psychologists who see themselves as both scientists and practitioners. But pressure has grown in recent years for greater recognition of the practitioner role. Among other things, this takes the form of a plea to psychologists to engage in activities which can be seen as directly relevant to societal problems. At the same time, the reward system remains heavily slanted towards more traditional and less obviously relevant approaches, e.g. academic promotion based on number of publications.

Institutional arrangements which would allow of greater specialization and training more directly geared to applied work would remove, or certainly reduce, many of the present tensions and conflicts. It would enable those with a flair for practice to concentrate on their applied work, without feeling compelled to justify their efforts to their scientific colleagues. Conversely, the latter would also have more elbow room for their own activities. The outcome could be more effective training at a graduate level, although it would entail students having to make a choice as to which mode of work they intend to enter. This scenario also presupposes an established career ladder for both groups.

In terms of deployment of resources there would be two distinct advantages. The cost of educational programmes would be cheaper, and they would be geared to producing the specialists sought by clients. In other words, this approach could lead to higher standards of professional competence. For such a development to take place, however, support from other bodies would be needed. Thus, any change of curriculum or training programmes within universities has immediate implication for the academic structure of the institution as a whole. Therefore, unless the revised programmes are acceptable to staff in other faculties, attempts at reform may fail. In addition, as the training programmes in most countries are financed from government sources any new programme will need the latter's support.

One disadvantage of early specialization and a career devoted to practice is that the individual may become too remote from theory and the scientific developments of the domain. Pragmatism is valuable only up to a point and, in the well-known words of Kurt Lewin, there is nothing so practical as a good theory. Likewise, scientists who are not challenged to consider the potential areas of application of their research run the dangers of becoming too abstract and highly theoretical.

The second possibility is almost the reverse of the first. Rather than separation, integration of the scientific and applied traditions is envisaged as part of an overall endeavour to make the profession more open, more relevant and with more ongoing dialogue between members and policy makers. It is not only work psychologists who are concerned with social issues, but the younger members of the profession as a whole are committed to a more proactive approach to these problems. Some of them are also much less concerned than their elders about the traditional distinctions between different branches of psychology. Throughout the profession, however, a more outgoing approach is evident in the sense that, rather than letting outside bodies and clients define the problem areas, psychologists perceive that they have a role to play in this process. It has become increasingly evident that, on the one hand, psychologists have not appreciated fully the constraints on policy makers, and on the other, that the latter have not understood the strength and limitations of the psychologists' activities.

Although the idea of a continuing dialogue is very attractive to many work psychologists, it will be difficult to implement in full. While it is comparatively easy to set up initial discussions, and indeed a number of psychologists and policy makers already confer informally on an individual basis, sustaining these initiatives is another matter. One reason for this is that policy makers, like managers, look for a pay-off in the relatively short term, which psychologists may not be able to provide. Another danger is that the discussions may become an end in themselves, rather than a means to an end, so that no action ensues. On the other hand, policy makers are now confronted with problems of such enormous complexity which often inhibit attempts at systematic exploration aimed at long-term solutions. Psychologists could contribute much to the diagnosis of these problems and the development of multidisciplinary programmes for action.

Before listing the advantages of this scenario, which are many, it should be noted that it is dependent on certain conditions being fulfilled. In the first place policy makers have to be convinced of the potential value of the approach and be willing to give access to information and resources. Convincing them probably depends on establishment figures in work psychology supporting this line of action, and being prepared to lobby for it and to participate in it. Secondly, it requires an integrated and strong professional organization which can manage the necessary interactions. The scale of research and development required is far greater than can be encompassed under present arrangements and the profession is inexperienced in operating this way.

An integrated approach, which encourages a maximum exchange between members of the profession and their clients, has the advantage that more cooperation and coordination should be possible, together with less duplication of effort. It also allows a more systematic problem solving approach, and may facilitate cooperation with other disciplines. Even if only partially implemented, the impact on society could be considerable, extending the acceptability of the profession and leading to more employment opportunities. It should also enhance the building up of knowledge, as theory is tested out in the solution of problems which, in turn, present new challenges to existing theory.

The chief disadvantage we see in this scenario is that it may be too big to be handled. It requires strong coordination of a kind in which members of the profession are inexperienced and a consensus amongst them on both means and ends, which may be very difficult to attain. As we noted earlier, work psychologists share common values only to a limited extent and there are many competing ideologies. Another difficulty may be that the ever-present tendency towards fragmentation of the field becomes intensified.

D.   Multidisciplinary approaches

Related to the above approach, but also distinct from it, is a future state in which work psychology develops within a multidisciplinary context. In this situation, the emphasis is upon the complementary nature of the work psychologists' contribution to those of other disciplines, such as industrial sociology, economics, operational research, political science and other subjects generally taught in schools of business and management. In certain countries, e.g. the USA, the large business schools already encompass this approach, but work psychologists employed in them identify with the domain of psychology rather than that of management or social science. However, faced with the complex problems of the present age, and the increasingly turbulent environment, some work psychologists feel that psychology cannot go it alone, and that they can make a more effective contribution as part of a multidisciplinary team.

There is an inherent attraction in this line of reasoning, which could lead to certain advantages. For example, it would decrease the competition and rivalry between disciplines and might encourage better use of resources. It would be less confusing to clients and sponsors, and would make for greater synergy and concentrated effort. In theory, integration should be easier, especially as members of other disciplines also welcome the idea of a multidisciplinary approach.

However, if this were to become the prevailing mode of activity, it would have significant consequences for the structuring of the domain and the profession. There would be a grave risk that other psychologists would no longer see work psychologists as professional colleagues but as a kind of hybrid. For work psychologists themselves, it could mean relinquishing some of the sources of identity on which they have come to rely, the strength of which, we suspect, is a good deal greater than many of us realize. One way in which traditional roots might be severed would be the transfer of graduate training of work psychologists from psychology departments to business schools and institutions of applied social science. It is probable that neither university departments nor professional organizations would welcome a move of this kind, which would reduce their membership. Therefore, although there are signs that the multidisciplinary approach may become a dominant ideology in the next few years, we think it is more likely to remain an ideal than to govern training and practice.

E. "Giving psychology away"

In his 1969 presidential address to the American Psychological Association, George Miller urged psychologists to discover how best to give psychology away, arguing that psychological knowledge should be passed freely to all who need and can use it. Only in this way did he feel that psychologists might contribute effectively to the promotion of human welfare.

As far as work psychology is concerned, quite a lot has been given away already. Over the past two decades, in some countries there has been a proliferation of popular books and journals aimed at the non-specialist reader describing, amongst other topics, theories of motivation at work, models of interpersonal and intergroup relations, leadership styles. Marked differences, however, exist between European countries. The mass media now present programmes with similar content and there is a widespread demand for lectures and short courses from a wide variety of occupational and interest groups.

However, members of the profession still distinguish between professionals and amateurs in that they do not consider all this dissemination of information qualifies the laity to practise as psychologists.

It is possible that these developments might be taken a good deal further in coming years, resulting in a better educated public and smaller gap between psychologists and non-psychologists. One can envisage a scenario in which the professional organization is weak, or even non-existent, and in which an increasing number of non-psychologists have a basic working knowledge of the subject, which they use in everyday affairs. This might follow the inclusion of psychology as part of the training programmes received by managers, personnel officers, trade union officials, administrators, social workers, engineers and other groups who perceive it as potentially useful to them. In these circumstances, the role of academic and professional psychologists might be likened to that of explorers and pioneers who are concerned with pushing forward the frontiers of the domain and extending the knowledge which is then expected to be passed to the widely dispersed body of lay practitioners.

The most obvious advantage of a development of this kind is that it would facilitate change, as a result of a better educated public aware of what psychology has to offer. Work psychologists could then no longer complain that their expertise was unknown and unappreciated as they would see others wanting to employ it on a "do it yourself basis". Indeed, given this situation, it is probable that psychologists would object that they were being left without a specialist function and, accordingly, would feel threatened.

The disadvantages of this scenario are more numerous. The risk of the abuse of knowledge and techniques, through ignorance rather than deliberate action, would be greatly increased. Likewise, it would be virtually impossible to identify the charlatans and to control the quality of work in the field as a whole. Giving away psychology is a one way traffic. Therefore, the psychologists themselves might soon become less sensitive to the problems, outlooks and values of those seeking to put psychology to use. Consequently, there could be a lack of fit between the psychologists' activities and society's needs. In terms of employment, opportunities for work psychologists *per se* would be limited. The content of their job would also be likely to alter to allow more attention to be given to the popularization of knowledge, a task which not all psychologists are able to undertake successfully. Neither of these developments are likely to be welcomed by members of the profession. There could also be consequences for the relationships with other disciplines, members of which form part of the wider group expecting to have access to and to make use of psychological knowledge. It is interesting to note that the history of psychology shows that ideas originating with psychologists are developed and applied by practitioners from other disciplines. To some extent this is due to the predominance of an academic career structure, leading to application and intervention being repeated as secondary activities. It is both a source of conflict and a contradiction that work psychologists like to regard themselves as equally at home in the world of their clients and academia, without recognizing that the career structure makes this virtually impossible.

F.   Retreat

Not all psychologists feel happy at the prospect of the kind of directions represented by the above scenarios. In particular, many find it difficult to sustain a sense of identity and purpose, or professional distinctiveness, when they are operating in situations in which there is a free exchange with lay people and members of other disciplines. This sense of discomfort is intensified when non-psychologists become interchangeable in certain work roles. As a result, there is a coping strategy of retreating to traditional areas of practice which are less readily accessible to non-psychologists, such as methodology, human factors and laboratory research.

Therefore, another scenario for the future is that we will see the development of this elitist outlook and the attempt to preserve the "purity" of work psychology separately from any multidisciplinary or generalist approaches. Coexisting with the movement towards cooperating and integration with others, we think it is likely that there may be a strengthening of traditionalism, e.g. concentrating on laboratory approaches.

One of the attractions of this course of action is that it provides work psychologists with an escape from the stresses of trying to live up to too high expectations on the part of both clients and themselves. Also, by concentrating on technocratic activities they can avoid confronting many social problems and identify with the role of the scientist, rather than that of the practitioner.

An advantage of this development would be the preservation of competence and expertise in the hands of competent small groups, so that the field represented by these specialist topics becomes clearly identifiable and manageable. This would be less confusing to clients, who would be assured of the well-substantiated basis of the services provided.

Likely disadvantages are a fragmentation of the field and isolation of the work psychologists concerned. Emphasis on techniques presupposes that, as in the early days, psychologists would respond to requests for their services, rather than participate in problems of definition or attempts at solution. Although we think there would be only a limited demand for these specialized activities, the possibility of a number of retreatist groups of this kind emerging in the next decade cannot be ignored.

G.   Withering away

The scenario of retreat described above could set in motion a process leading to the demise of work psychology altogether. This could occur if the activities of work psychologists cease to appear relevant, both to other members of the scientific community, and to clients and policy makers. Such a process of gradual decay may be very insidious, in that it may not be easy to detect the extent to which work psychologists are becoming ignored by consumers. Thus members of the profession may continue to reinforce each other's activities, in the conviction that these are still appropriate and right, while ignoring the signs that society at large is paying less and less attention to what they are doing. In our view, some of the accounts given in Section 2 of this book illustrate the process of erosion which has occurred in some countries. It should be emphasized that withering away is the consequence of others' evaluation of work psychology, rather more than psychologists' own activities. For the individual practitioner it is very difficult to distinguish what is adaptive behaviour to changing circumstances from what is outmoded practice, especially if the latter is supported by relevant peer groups. Equally important in this connection may be the failure to engage in political and marketing activities to ensure preservation of the work psychologists' territory in the face of competition from other groups. To counteract the danger inherent in this scenario it is necessary that work psychologists have a sensitive appreciation of the environment in which they are working. It is not sufficient to assume that because certain clients continue to support them, or that certain activities are still in demand, that these will continue for many years to come. Signs of declining interests on the part of consumers need to be taken seriously and investigated to see whether they are transitory phenomena or the portents of more far-reaching changes.

H.   Opting out

Another response to the conflicts and contradictions we have discussed earlier is that of opting out of psychology altogether. This is usually an individualistic rather than a collective reaction, but it is possible that if a sufficient number of people make this choice it could create a bandwagon effect. The likelihood of this occurring clearly depends on circumstances, but it will be enhanced in countries where work psychologists tend to be employed as individuals and are cut off from close contact with professional colleagues. We recognize that, for certain individuals, there may be strategic advantage in ceasing to claim the professional role of psychology and adopting an occupational position and title which gives them greater freedom of action. Some examples are those who find it expedient to call themselves management development or organizational development specialists or public relations officers, and so on. In particular contexts this can lead to reduction of dissonance for employers, practitioners and clients alike.

It is difficult to assess the possible extent of such opting out and the consequences for the profession. Clearly, however, the latter would be weakened if several work psychologists felt that their interests lay more outside the profession than within it. In that case, a situation could also develop easily in which there ceased to be any clear relationship between training, research and practice.

I. External interventions

As the environment of work psychologists impinges more and more on their activities, as exemplified by employment legislation, government policies and so on, it is possible that external forces might come to dominate developments in the domain, and render the profession itself relatively powerless. There are two main ways in which external forces may exert strong influences. The first is through the control of resources. As we have already indicated, a very large proportion of the total educational and research effort in most countries is financed by government agencies, which therefore have the power to control the direction of future developments. Secondly, regardless of whatever political party is in office, it is clear that there is a move away from any type of *laissez-faire* administration towards more centralized control and systematic planning. The consequences of this are that public and private sector organizations, as well as individuals and groups, have much less freedom of choice than formerly, as their activities become subject to more intervention from without. An example which has been given prominence in recent years is that of employment legislation, particularly that pertaining to the employment of women, racial minorities and disabled groups.

An unattractive scenario for the future, therefore, which is not outside the boundaries of possibility, is that work psychologists may lose control over the development of their domain. This could take the form of being required to train more or fewer students than they wish, perhaps with inadequate resources, or to engage in inappropriate programmes which have been designed by others. It could also mean that funds are not available for the research which psychologists see as important, but only for those projects which government and sponsoring bodies are prepared to commission.

J. Concluding comments

Reflection on these scenarios leads to some stark conclusions. The first of these is that, whether we like it or not, as work psychologists we have to operate as politicians, not only in taking initiatives to extend our spheres of influence but also in defending the domain. Claims of professional competence cannot be substantiated scientifically, but have to be agreed and negotiated in interactions with other members of the profession, outside bodies and other disciplines. Outside the laboratory, it is not possible to function solely as a scientist because one is caught up in a problem-orientated environment in which there are many competing and conflicting interests. Secondly, work psychology is no longer in its infancy, although the suggestion that it is may still be given as an excuse when looking at the comparatively little impact made by many psychological interventions and applications. If some of the success stories of the 1960s have not endured into the late 1970s, it behoves us to seek to understand why and to accept both our strengths and limitations.

In presenting these various scenarios we have tried to be as objective as possible, looking at the field as we see it in our respective countries and in those of our co-contributors. In each instance we have sought to identify positive and negative aspects of a possible future, although others may see the situation differently. It is desirable that these issues are discussed as widely as possible throughout the profession in order to test the strength and validity of our interpretations. We shall not refrain from raising such issues ourselves in professional circles as we feel that they are too important to be disregarded.

One of the major contradictions which has emerged from our review of the European scene is the rate of growth of the domain, on the one hand, which gives rise to a sense of optimism, and the weakness of work psychology as a profession on the other, which engenders pessimism. In all countries the growth of training programmes and the diversification of research and interventions can be clearly seen, and the number of publications in work psychology continues to grow. There is also a far greater penetration of work psychology with other social sciences than previously and a beneficial exchange of concepts across disciplinary boundaries. This has to be set against the identity problems of work psychologists as practitioners, which we described earlier, of which one symptom is that clients are no longer sure, nor are they particularly concerned, as to whether they are seeking the help of a psychologist or some other expert. We also have the impression that some important and prospective clients, e.g. many senior executives, union officers and government administrators, have little faith in what we have to offer, looking to others for the kind of help which work psychologists ought to be able to provide.

Many work psychologists themselves appear to be very uncertain about their position, which is why most of the scenarios are not very encouraging. Although the situation varies throughout Europe, it seems true to say that work psychologists are not much of a force to be reckoned with in any one country. We suggest that one of the reasons for this paradox lies in the dominant faction of work psychologists being located in academia rather than in the field itself. Hence the tension, which exists in any profession (Mok, 1973), between those who seek to advance knowledge and those who are practitioners pulls psychologists towards scientific activity rather than finding the best way of coping with client problems. This contrasts with, for example, the medical profession in which problems encountered in practice lead to subsequent academic research rather than the other way round. Too little account seems to have been taken of the different patterns of reinforcement which operate in universities and outside them. Thus, young work psychologists are socialized by their training to become research scientists and are not taught to take responsibility for diagnosis and remedial actions, within financial and time constraints and in conflicting situations, as is expected of them in applied organizational work. This source of professional weakness is unlikely to change as long as the present appointment and promotion system in universities persists, whereby performance as a scientist and number of publications are the main criteria considered. In non-academic institutions, particularly in industry, reinforcement patterns are quite different, and the work psychologist who points out the multiple variables operating in a given situation is likely to get shortshrift from executives, who want to be given a prescription for immediate activities. It is not part of work psychologists' expectations that they should do more than diagnose and investigate problems, so there is a shock effect when their carefully prepared analyses are rejected by clients as inappropriate.

We shall now indicate what our own preferences are for future developments, and consider what will be needed to achieve these desirable objectives. We will try to analyse both the constraints and opportunities facing us, recognizing fully that there is no one best way which can be prescribed for work psychologists in all countries.

Our own preferred recommendation for the future would be some combination of "reform from within" and a "multidisciplinary approach" leading to a different image of the profession. However, we recognize that the extent to which this might come about depends not only on work psychologists but on the subject as a whole, and the much larger number of psychologists specializing in other branches of the subject. Psychologists do not identify strongly with each other, in the sense of defending and supporting the corporate image of their discipline when this is under attack from outside. For example clinical psychologists do not defend work psychologists, when criticized, and vice versa. It seems to us that work psychologists delude themselves if they think they can operate independently as a professional group because, despite the growth in recent years, they do not cohere sufficiently, nor are they numerically strong enough to exert influence outside the existing national and international organizations.

We would like to make some speculative suggestions about possible ways forward. These range from initiatives which may have to be taken at an individual level to those which would require governmental support or the backing of international bodies. In all instances the emphasis is on continuing dialogue, both within and outside the profession, as distinct from the prevailing pattern of formal and intermittent conferences and consultations. Within each country it seems desirable that work psychologists who are aware of the problems we have described should seek to be more proactive in promoting the profession. In many cases there is a tendency to wait until asked, rather than taking the initiative in engaging with others to seek solutions to contemporary problems. For example, comparatively few psychologists are involved in the design of systems and therefore can do little about many problems arising from technological decisions made earlier. This leads to a restrictive view on the part of both clients and work psychologists themselves about what the profession has to offer. Work psychologists must be prepared to consort with engineers, managers, architects, and other experts in order to appreciate the parameters within which these other experts operate. They also need to educate potential clients and consumers about the nature of the domain. In this connection it is interesting to note that there is at least one European industrial sociologist who writes regularly for a national newspaper about work structuring.

The multifaceted nature of organizational problems is now generally recognized. However, although multidisciplinary approaches to deal with these problems are commonly advocated, in practice this often means experts working in parallel with one another, rather than interactively. In our view some pioneering work is needed by members of the profession to discover ways of developing effective information exchange, and modes of cooperation with other disciplines. This will entail more than a sharing of concepts or the development of a common frame of reference: there is a need for active research and development in its own right to discover how those schooled in different disciplines can communicate with one another. Advanced technology presents the world with many choices for which no precedents exist, so that it is possible that this will favour the collaborative exchange between disciplines envisaged here. Within some countries too, it is not unreasonable that more government support might be sought for development. To date the relationships between government bodies and work psychologists is usually confined to the support of scientific research, with occasional advice being sought from the professional association on specific issues. Strengthening of the practitioners could be achieved more effectively and possibly more swiftly if government agencies were to support training and development directed to this end. The professional associations themselves would also exert an important influence if they were seen to give more active endorsement to the practitioner's role.

Although facilities exist for the exchange of scholars between different countries, this is usually arranged on an individual basis, and in competition with other disciplines for the funds available. We feel that the process of dialogue would be greatly facilitated if not only those with established reputations, but graduate students and young faculty members could spend short or longer periods in working with their peers in other countries. To achieve this it may be necessary to establish some information centre or network to inform people of the opportunities available, and of the kind of work being carried out in different centres. The degree of ignorance of what is taking place even within one's own country, let alone in other European countries, should not be underestimated. Perhaps a start might be made by the professional organizations, both national and international, exchanging information sheets about the activities of work psychologists. Looking at the European scene as a whole, it strikes us that if we were free to recommend where specialists in a particular area of work psychology, e.g. ergonomics or workstructuring, could learn at first hand from those at the forefront of the field they would not necessarily be trained in their own country. "Centres of excellence" are not confined to any one nation, and the attempt to establish them in all branches of the subject in every country is a waste of limited resources. The domain would benefit if it became customary that advanced training and graduate work in a particular subspecialism were undertaken at institutes with a renowned reputation, even though this means that some students will have to become bilingual.

More interesting in the context of this volume are the possibilities provided by the setting up of informal and formal multinational taskgroups of work psychologists. The former are those arising from existing friendships and chance contacts made at international conferences and elsewhere, whereby a small number of work psychologists come together by mutual agreement to prepare a paper or to undertake research. As Hakel observes in Chapter 16, a common task is a necessary but not a sufficient condition for the development of such multinational peer groups. For this reason they can also be formed by funding bodies with an interest in comparative research and the prompting of exchange of scholars between countries. However, it is essential that such groups are small enough to encourage optimal interaction between the members who, in turn, need to be committed to the task and not see group membership in terms of status or elitism. Our experience is that the benefits and unforeseen pay-offs of such groups far exceed any costs in time, distance and language problems. We would like to recommend that ways of promoting such peer groups be explored.

Another type of multinational group which we would like to see encouraged would be that including in its membership work psychologists from developing countries and the Third World, who often have no immediate peer groups to support them. Practitioners in the developed countries increasingly are confronted with problems located in other parts of the world, through their students from overseas, through contacts with multinational organizations, teaching and examining for universities in other countries, and similar activities. European experience is not always pertinent to other cultures, and the implicit values and assumptions of much theory and practice in work psychology are too strongly rooted in the United States and Western European traditions to have universal application. Here again some experimental developmental work is needed to discover the appropriate balance of membership in such a group between those from the West and the East, and from both northern and southern hemispheres, from different national and cultural outlooks. To the best of our knowledge this type of enterprise does not exist at present, but it is one which might well attract funding in future.

References

McCollum, I. M. (1960). Psychologists in industry in the United Kingdom and Western Germany. *American Psychologist,* 15, 58-64.
Miller, G. A. (1969). Psychology as a means of promoting human welfare. *American Psychologist,* 1968, 24, 1063-1075.
Mok, A. L. (1973). *Beroepen in Actie.* Boom, Meppel.

Subject Index